DECRYPTING MONEY

DECRYPTING MONEY

A COMPREHENSIVE INTRODUCTION TO BITCOIN

MARCO KROHN, ANTHONY JEFFERIES,
MARCO STRENG, AND ZORAN BALKIC

DECRYPTING MONEY
A Comprehensive Introduction to Bitcoin

FIRST EDITION

ISBN   978-1-5445-3598-2 *Hardcover*

          978-1-5445-3599-9 *Paperback*

          978-1-5445-3600-2 *Ebook*

CONTENTS

Bitcoin
Genesis Block
Raw Hex

```
00000000  01 00 00 00 00 00 00 00 00 00 00 00 00 00 00 00  |................|
00000010  00 00 00 00 00 00 00 00 00 00 00 00 00 00 00 00  |................|
00000020  00 00 00 00 3B A3 ED FD 7A 7B 12 B2 7A C7 2C 3E  |....;...z{..z.,>|
00000030  67 76 8F 61 7F C8 1B C3 88 8A 51 32 3A 9F B8 AA  |gv.a......Q2:...|
00000040  4B 1E 5E 4A 29 AB 5F 49 FF FF 00 1D 1D AC 2B 7C  |z{..z.,>gv.a....|
00000050  01 01 00 00 00 01 00 00 00 00 00 00 00 00 00 00  |......+|........|
00000060  00 00 00 00 00 00 00 00 00 00 00 00 00 00 00 00  |................|
00000070  00 00 00 00 00 00 FF FF FF FF 4D 04 FF FF 00 1D  |................|
00000080  01 04 45 54 68 65 20 54 69 6D 65 73 20 30 33 2F  |..M.......EThe T|
00000090  4A 61 6E 2F 32 30 30 39 20 43 68 61 6E 63 65 6C  |imes  03/Jan/2009|
000000A0  6C 6F 72 20 6F 6E 20 62 72 69 6E 6B 20 6F 66 20  |Chancellor on b |
000000B0  73 65 63 6F 6E 64 20 62 61 69 6C 6F 75 74 20 66  |rink of second b |
000000C0  6F 72 20 62 61 6E 6B 73 FF FF FF FF 01 00 F2 05  |ailout for banks|
000000D0  2A 01 00 00 00 43 41 04 67 8A FD B0 FE 55 48 27  |........*....CA.|
000000E0  19 67 F1 A6 71 30 B7 10 5C D6 A8 28 E0 39 09 A6  |g....UH'.g..q0..|
000000F0  79 62 E0 EA 1F 61 DE B6 49 F6 BC 3F 4C EF 38 C4  |\..(.9..yb...a.|
```

Hash
000000000019d6689c085ae165831e934ff763ae46a2a6c172b3f1b60a8ce26f

Merkle root
4a5e1e4baab89f3a32518a88c31bc87f618f76673e2cc77ab2127b7afdeda33b

Address
1A1zP1eP5QGefi2DMPTfTL5SLmv7DivfNa

Timestamp	Block Height	Difficulty	Version
2009-01-03 19:15	0	1.00	0x1

Bits	Weight	Size	Nonce
486,604,799	1,140 WU	285 bytes	2,083,236,893

Miner	TX Volume	Block Reward	Fee Reward
Unknown	0 BTC	50 BTC	0 BTC

Figure 0.1: The first block of the bitcoin blockchain contains the text "The Times 03/Jan/2009 Chancellor on brink of second bailout for banks." A reference to the headline of The Times of that day left by the mysterious bitcoin inventor who called himself "Satoshi Nakamoto." The block itself was "mined" at 6:15 p.m. (GMT) on January 3, 2009.

Please visit our website www.decryptingmoney.com for further information about the book and our contact details.

FOREWORD

by Garry Kasparov

LET ME PRESENT A THOUGHT EXPERIMENT: IMAGINE YOU ARE a dissident fighting for democracy in Venezuela. The government controls access to financial services through state institutions. Those loyal to the regime have access to the nation's scant resources. Dissidents like yourself are locked out. The government monitors your every move, tracking what financial transactions you are allowed to make and chasing your footprints (both digital and physical) everywhere. What can you do? How can you survive and continue to speak out?

And what if the government also manipulates the national currency, printing money and playing with its value, trying—like Nero declaring war against Neptune—to wage war against economics itself? Can that be called stable? How can a company or family plan for the future when the basic block of saving, spending, and investment is subject to the whims and abuses of a malign ruler?

But this is not merely a thought experiment. This is real life, for both dissidents and ordinary people all around the world. One answer to this problem is cryptocurrency like bitcoin. For countless people around the world, in an age of ever greater control and surveillance, crypto means freedom.

I realize this may sound like an edge case, and specific to my advocacy as the chairman of the Human Rights Foundation. But most new technology first finds such fringe applications before becoming broadly understood and utilized in the mainstream. Early adopters take on risk, encounter challenges, and pave the way for the rest.

That's where cryptocurrency is today, and we are lucky to have a book like *Decrypting Money* to help us move into the next phase. Placing bitcoin in the historical context of all currency—back to seashells!—is similar to the comparisons of the internet to the printing press.

I've always been obsessed with new tech, from my matches against chess supercomputers to lecturing about how AI will become augmented intelligence by making us smarter. Exploration has been one of my core values my whole life, even before chess. From tracing the paths of the great explorers on a globe with my father to taking on new challenges in my personal and professional lives, exploring is learning. Exploring means taking the road less traveled, often bumpy and lacking proper signage. It changes the way we think and, if we share our explorations, also changes the world around us.

So I was an eager audience when I met Marco Streng in spring 2019, recognizing him as a fellow explorer. I'm also a natural skeptic, however, so his passion for the subject of cryptocurrency wasn't enough to convince me. It was his desire to look beyond the hype of the moment, all the speculation and the myths, to present coherent plans and prospects for "internet money" in the near and distant future.

This wasn't only my habit of always looking a dozen moves ahead. My motto has always been to think big and be optimistic—but always have a plan. The authors of this book take context and planning seriously, realizing that this foundation is even more important than cool tech and social buzz when the goal is to change the world. And what could be a bigger change than reshaping the entire global economic relationship with money, from megabanks to food cart vendors, from dissidents to presidents?

I spend much of my time today thinking and writing about the intersection of rights and technology. Free speech in the internet age, for example, along with data ownership, privacy, and cybersecurity. In every case, tech has created endless possibilities, including new threats and exploits, just like nearly every new technology throughout history.

Cryptocurrency is no exception, so it's critical to have a broader understanding of what it is and what it is not—and what it will one day be. Usually we speak of the past with certainty, the present with confidence, and the future with doubt. With bitcoin it is quite different. Its origin was unspectacular and its creator is still mysterious. Its present is ferociously debated, with extremes of curse and blessing. This is a status reserved only for the most powerful influences—again I refer to the printing press and the internet. As I often point out about artificial intelligence, our tech is agnostic, neither good nor evil. It's how we use it.

But bitcoin's future, there I am convinced. It IS the future, one where we will look back at our current bills, coins, and central banking standards the way we look back at those seashells today. I'm not sure I'll live to see it, although I hope I will, because it will indicate that so many other positive transformations in personal freedom and societal change have come to pass. Cryptocurrency isn't only on the cutting edge of technology, but also of human rights and the relationships between government, private enterprise, and individuals. As such, its success is a bellwether for human progress.

My gratitude to the authors for illuminating my path on this bumpy and exciting road, and I'm sure you will enjoy the ride as well. Just turn the page.

Garry Kasparov
Chairman, Human Rights Foundation
Chairman, Renew Democracy Initiative
13th World Chess Champion
New York City

INTRODUCTION

THE ORIGIN OF THIS BOOK STEMS FROM OUR INDIVIDUAL stories of how we first encountered bitcoin. We would have almost certainly never met each other without bitcoin, and none of us could have imagined how life-changing bitcoin would be for us. Between 2011 and 2013, we all separately and in rather different ways were introduced to, learned about, and became involved with this cryptocurrency. Marco Krohn's summary of his earliest experiences with bitcoin moves from initial skepticism to a changed perspective on economics, the nature of money, and tremendous business opportunities.

Marco first learned about virtual currency one afternoon in the summer of 2011 from what he was expecting to be the least interesting article in a computer magazine. That day, he read that a mysterious, anonymous figure had invented internet money and that anyone with adequate computer skills could generate more. He had a PhD in theoretical physics, a job in the banking industry, and an opinion: The idea was crazy. It couldn't work.

This was, he remembered the next day, the same opinion he'd had when he first heard about Wikipedia. Somewhat humbled by the recollection, he gave bitcoin a deeper look, and fell right down the rabbit hole.[1] The more he understood, the more intrigued he became. The core principles, while not immediately obvious, were fundamentally solid, and the implications profound. The idea *was* crazy—like vaccination and heliocentricity had been. Eleven years and the founding of one of the world's largest bitcoin mining companies later, he is even more convinced that this new form of money will be as significant as the microprocessor to individual, commercial, and world economies.

He gave up his banking job and, with a few friends, soon had a server farm set up and running in Bosnia-Herzegovina. A single cavernous room full of graphic cards and computers with constellations of blinking lights, it looked (and sounded) like a spaceship—and friends reacted to it in much the same way. Over and over, Marco and his partners found themselves explaining that their futuristic, noisy warehouse was "printing money." And almost every time, people wanted in.

In the beginning the bitcoin community was small, full of people who had similar experiences and stories about how they discovered bitcoin. Anthony Jefferies, Marco Streng,

---

1 Bitcoin is both a currency and a payment system. Initially, this distinction was reflected using upper- and lowercase versions of the letter "B," such that "bitcoin" meant the currency (as in, "I owe two bitcoins"), while "Bitcoin" referred to the system itself (as in, "I can use Bitcoin to transfer your money"). That convention has largely fallen out of use within the bitcoin community, and we use the lowercase "b" exclusively.

Zoran Balkic, and Marco Krohn met in these early days, and were thrilled about bitcoin's potentially wide-reaching implications.

That desire, they came to see, went well beyond their extended circle. A keen and growing population was interested in bitcoin. People had a tantalizing sense of fortunes being made on just the other side of some obscure information barrier and were frustrated that they didn't understand what it did or how to participate.

In the same way that the power of personal computing needed a graphic interface to make it accessible to laypeople, bitcoin (or more generally "cryptocurrency") needs an intermediary. Here, the necessary layer between humans and technology is informational rather than visual. People need a conceptual handhold on what cryptocurrency is and how it operates before they can interact with it effectively. However, unlike computers, which few people had experience with even fifty years ago, money is a tool we are confident everyone reading already uses regularly. Unfortunately, familiarity isn't the same as understanding. In fact, it can get in the way.

Money is an incredibly useful abstraction that has evolved with human culture from shells on beaches to chips on cards, with each iteration improving if not perfecting it. Cryptocurrency exacts an intellectual and conceptual toll, asking an ante of intelligence and imagination of its participants.

If you ask the average person what money is, many will say it's the bills in their wallets. When we first heard about bitcoin, our level of understanding wasn't much more sophisticated, although we have degrees in mathematics or engineering, or worked in a bank!! We could understand and marvel at the math and coding behind bitcoin, but not until we learned more about the history, functions, and properties of money did we fully appreciate the true genius of bitcoin or recognize how profound and far-reaching its consequences could be.

TOWARD A DEEPER UNDERSTANDING

Bitcoin doesn't have to be arcane, but books on the subject tend toward either the simplistic or the extremely technical. While there's a lot of good information online, it can be difficult to find both a high-level overview and a sufficient level of detail combined in the same place. In 2013, when we realized bitcoin's mathematical and conceptual complexities separated our friends and too many other interested non-experts from the chance to invest in (and profit from) bitcoin mining, we founded Genesis Mining to bridge that gap. This book is an extension of that bridge.

Through this book, we hope to share our excitement, to provide a direct path to a deeper level of understanding—skirting the most technically complex aspects of bitcoin without oversimplifying more than is necessary. This is neither an "Idiot's Guide" nor a university-level text on cryptocurrencies and blockchains. Rather, it's a comprehensive introduction for interested, intelligent laypeople who want to understand how this new "internet money" is used and made, and perhaps to make some of it for themselves.

To give readers a similar grounding, Part One of *Decrypting Money* provides an exploration of money, beginning, in Chapter 1, with one of its earliest forms—the cowry shell—and continuing through the rise of government-issued paper currency. This is not a comprehensive history, but a historically ordered representative sample of currencies chosen, in part, for their ability to illustrate those functions and traits of money that are the focus of Chapter 2.

Chapter 3 covers the evolution of digital currency, evaluates it by the functions and traits detailed in the previous chapter, and compares it with the example historical currencies from the first chapter. This will establish that (non-physical) digital money can have the traits and properties that in principle allow it to be used as (a digital form of) money. Part One concludes with an exploration of problems inherent to all forms of money and an overview of how several early digital currencies attempted to address some of these.

Part Two focuses on bitcoin, the original cryptocurrency. Chapter 4 begins with the mystery of Satoshi Nakamoto (the alias of the unknown person or people who invented bitcoin), his agenda, and his genius. It covers bitcoin's introduction and early history, from the initial white paper through the famous bitcoin pizza, which is considered to be the most expensive pizza in the history of humankind.[2] In Chapter 5, we analyze bitcoin by the functions and traits of money that have been established. Finally, we compare it with the predominant money forms of our time, gold and fiat, and discuss its relative strengths and weaknesses.

---

2 A white paper is an in-depth document that describes a specific topic.

Chapter 6 is an introduction to bitcoin fundamentals, introducing and explaining concepts like addresses, public-private keys, ledgers, wallets, exchanges, nodes, and mining. This chapter provides succinct explanations of the two primary ways people can start using bitcoin. This overview of bitcoin wallets, exchanges, ATMs, and mining provides high-level descriptions to help readers orient and protect themselves in the bitcoin landscape.

Part Three digs deeper into how bitcoin works. Chapter 7 provides a more in-depth, technical discussion of the cryptographic functions on which bitcoin depends. Chapter 8 focuses on how transactions are authenticated and new bitcoins are created, as well as explaining the blockchain: what it is, how it operates, and what both protects it and ensures its continuation. Part Three ends with Chapter 8's description of the key process by which bitcoin is created: mining.

BOTH PHILOSOPHY AND CURRENCY

Bitcoin is more than a currency. It began as an almost philosophical conversation on a cypherpunk mailing list about what a better form of money would look like, and its origin shaped both it and its initial audience.[3] That early demographic continues to comprise a significant portion of the people (and particularly the people most heavily) involved in bitcoin. This cohort is the cypherpunks. They come to bitcoin from an interest in cryptography and place a high premium on protecting individual privacy.

---

3 "Cypherpunk" is derived from the words "cipher" and "cyberpunk."

Privacy is necessary for an open society in the electronic age. Privacy is not secrecy. A private matter is something one doesn't want the whole world to know, but a secret matter is something one doesn't want anybody to know. Privacy is the power to selectively reveal oneself to the world.[4]

Cypherpunks are attracted by both the underlying philosophy of bitcoin and a method of transferring value that does not require them to reveal their identities. These people tend to be antiauthoritarian and distrustful of the state and traditional forms of government. For them, bitcoin is an ideology almost as much as it is a currency. It's certainly a community.

The second demographic to enter the bitcoin community comprises what we think of as "gold bugs" and libertarians.[5] These are people who believe that scarcity and value are inextricably linked. They have an inherent belief in bitcoin because it is (and will always be) scarce, and a deep distrust of fiat money because it is neither scarce nor backed by anything that is. This group shares a distrust of the state with the cypherpunks but tends to be much more heavily invested in gold than their counterparts and less ideologically driven. For this group, bitcoin is a digital form of gold, and they buy it as a way of diversifying their precious metal holdings.

---

4   Eric Hughes, "A Cypherpunk's Manifesto," Activism.net, March 9, 1993, https://www.activism.net/cypherpunk/manifesto.html.

5   Libertarians hold liberty as their core value. They are skeptical of any authority or state power.

Another group, the speculators, are attracted by bitcoin's price history—from a percentage of a cent to thousands of dollars per bitcoin—and are hoping to get in on a rising tide and make a great deal of money quickly.

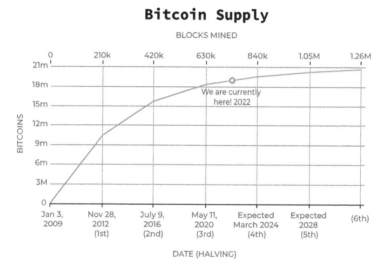

Figure 0.2: Bitcoin supply curve

While we have striven for objectivity in this book and encourage readers to seek information about bitcoin from a variety of other sources, we felt a responsibility to provide context about the different perspectives and biases that predominate in the bitcoin culture and to be explicit about where we position ourselves among them.

This brief demographic survey also helps explain some of the movement in the bitcoin market. Price spikes tend to attract an influx of new speculator market participants trying to exploit the rapid change in the price to make money very quickly.

The volatility of bitcoin is one of both its attractions and its risks. We can't predict the future, and that's not the purpose of this book. Rather, its goal is to communicate the fundamental principles of bitcoin and other cryptocurrencies, so that you are able to assess these important emerging technologies on your own.

ABOUT US

This book is a collaboration. All of us have worked at the forefront of cryptocurrency and blockchain technologies since their earliest days and have founded and run companies based in that dynamic environment. But we each came to it from different backgrounds and with different strengths:

Marco Krohn's knowledge about blockchain technology and cryptocurrencies benefits from his advanced studies in physics, mathematics, and economics, as well as over a decade of experience working in finance and investment banking. When he's not working, Marco enjoys reading about new technologies. At heart, he is a tech junkie with an appreciation for clever, simple solutions. Marco especially enjoys learning of advancements in applied sciences that are both elegant and profound in their potential to radically improve the way people live their lives. Marco is from northern Germany and holds a PhD in theoretical physics.

With degrees in mathematics and engineering, as well as a PhD in computational fluid dynamics, Anthony Jefferies had already encountered some of the relevant concepts when he arrived at bitcoin, such as public-key cryptography and distributed computing. Since then, he has been involved in a number of cryptocurrency projects, including a cryptocurrency exchange and the development of quantitative tools for bitcoin data analysis. He also worked for more than ten years at major German car manufacturers carrying out numerical simulations for the research and development division.

Marco Streng discovered bitcoin as a young math prodigy studying emerging and self-organizing networks and was immediately attracted to its complexities and opportunities. He began mining in his student dorm room, before scaling up his operation into what became Genesis Mining.

Zoran Balkic has been a computer scientist since he was a child, and studied and then taught computer science at university for fifteen years. His first bitcoin project in 2013 involved using SMS to buy bitcoin, and he went on to found and lead successful companies in the cryptocurrency industry. His interest in education continues, and he is an active participant in the Croatian bitcoin community.

Each of us had our own "down the rabbit hole" moment, and we're all still as enthusiastic about the possibilities it opens up as we were then. Cryptocurrency, the ideas behind it, the mathematics and technology on which it relies, and the proliferation of new varieties can seem impenetrably complex and abstract, but bitcoin is simply the next logical step in the evolution of money. To better understand that evolution, we start as close to its beginning as we can—with a seashell.

We can't promise Alice's wonderland, but we hope you'll enjoy the ride.

PART 1

THE HISTORY
OF MONEY

1

THE ORIGINS OF MONEY

IS BITCOIN MONEY? ARE OTHER CRYPTOCURRENCIES? BEFORE answering these fundamental questions, we've got to get clear on what precisely money is. For that, in this chapter we study examples of the very diverse types of money that humankind invented. In the process we learn about its properties, and also in many cases why a currency eventually failed.

Most people have earned, spent, and saved money since we were old enough for the tooth fairy and a piggy bank, and some form of it has been a part of every human civilization since before we worked metal. Many people seem to have a vague sense of money's origins—some imagined, hazy prehistory in which a primitive barter system evolved into a crude currency to mediate between the value of a chicken and a pair of shoes. It's an intuitive view promulgated (without evidence) by the otherwise fairly rigorous Adam Smith in his famous *The Wealth of Nations*.

In fact, while everything from snail shells to cigarettes has taken a turn as currency, there is little ethnographic evidence that a barter economy ever existed, much less evolved into a currency-based one.[6] Rather, money seems to have been an abstraction from the beginning, and its history is full of surprises.

1. COMMODITY MONEY

Perhaps the least abstract form of currency, commodity money is itself useful and of intrinsic value. Distinct from barter, in which goods are traded against other goods, commodity money is a commonly agreed-upon good that serves an additional function as a medium of exchange.[7] Albert might be able to barter a table for a cow and a cow for a new pair of boots, but if the cobbler doesn't need beef, Albert goes shoeless. If, however, cows are also a currency, the shoemaker would accept Bessie confident he will be able to purchase the lumber he needs, since everyone takes cows as payment.

1.i. Cowry Shells

Perhaps the oldest—and certainly one of the longest-lived—forms of currency, the small oval shells of a species of sea snails (*Cypraea moneta*) are so deeply associated with money

---

6 "No example of a barter economy, pure and simple, has ever been described, let alone the emergence from it of money; all available ethnography suggests that there never has been such a thing." [Caroline Humphrey, "Barter and Economic Disintegration," *Man* 20, no. 1 (March 1985): 48, https://doi.org/10.2307/2802221.]

7 See Chapter 2.1.i.

and trade in China that the evocative 貝 cowry symbol is part of the written form of many Chinese words with commercial and financial implications, such as wealth (財) and account (賬).[8] In use from as early as the fourth century BC through the twentieth century, and throughout North America, Africa, Asia, and Oceania, the cowry owes its longevity and widespread use to several critical characteristics. In addition to the function it shares with gold and silver as personal ornamentation, the cowry shell is small and lightweight, which makes it easy to handle and transport. Its organic intricacy renders it difficult to counterfeit, while its uniformity of size makes it possible to assess multiples by weight, eliminating the time-consuming work of counting each individually.

Figure 1.1: Cowry shells, perhaps the oldest form of currency (Source: Bin im Garten, "Monetaria annulus 00101," Wikimedia Commons, last modified June 19, 2020, https://commons. wikimedia.org/wiki/File:Monetaria_annulus_0010.JPG.)

---

8 Bin Yang, *Cowrie Shells and Cowrie Money: A Global History* (New York: Routledge, 2019), 140.

1.ii. Rai Stones

As a fascinating point of contrast to easily divisible, portable shell money, the stone currency of the Yap Islands can weigh up to four tons. Made of limestone, which is not native there, rai stones were hand-carved into flattened discs or doughnut shapes through tremendous investments of time and labor. The stones were mined and shaped on Palau, an island 450 kilometers (280 miles) away and transported by canoe at considerable risk to life and limestone.

In fact, the value of an individual stone was enhanced by both difficulty and danger. A stone of the same size, shape, and weight was worth more if someone died on the journey from Palau to Yap. The social rank of the people involved in a stone's creation and the story of its steadily accumulating history also added to (or detracted from) its worth. They were rarely used in financial transactions and, as such, were less a currency than a physical manifestation of value.

While they ranged from the diameter of a D battery to taller than the average elephant (and as heavy), their ownership was not established by possession (they rarely changed physical location) but by declaration. As a result, true theft was impossible. A ne'er-do-well might steal Stan's stone, but if its transfer from Stan to the would-be thief had not been proclaimed aloud to everyone, and its change of ownership made an official part of the island's oral history, having physical possession of his money did nothing to decrease Stan's wealth or enhance the thief's. This level of abstraction became so sophisticated that, its ownership having been recorded, one massive rai stone continued to be treated as usable currency when it sank to the bottom of the ocean on its journey from Palau.[9]

Figure 1.2: Rai stones, valued for their weight and history (Source: Eric Guinther, "Yap Stone Money," Wikimedia Commons, last modified December 28, 2020, https://commons.wikimedia.org/wiki/File:Yap_Stone_Money.jpg.)

It's unclear when the carving of rai stones began, but at one point, up to 10 percent of the Yap Islands' adult male population was engaged in their carving and transportation. This work, and indeed the economy of the entire culture, changed

9 Jacob Goldstein and David Kestenbaum, "The Island of Stone Money," NPR, December 10, 2010, https://www.npr.org/sections/money/2011/02/15/131934618/the-island-of-stone-money.

in 1871 when David Dean O'Keefe was shipwrecked on the island, introducing iron tools and large sailing vessels, which dramatically increased the speed at which the rai stones could be carved and transported. This influx of iron-carved and easily transported stones drove such aggressive inflation that the islanders came to value them less, while older stones, new ones carved the old way, or stones obtained with great difficulty and peril experienced a relative increase in value.[10]

1.iii. Roman Denarii

An excellent early example of a government-controlled currency, the denarius, was the keystone silver coin of the Roman Empire for the approximately 450 years between 211 BC and 240 AD. In 15 BC, Caesar Augustus issued a decree standardizing the denarius.[11] He set its weight at 3.9 grams and mandated a coin with a silver content of 95 to 98 percent.[12] This formalization replaced the use of coins of various sizes and compositions whose value had been exclusively determined by weight.

---

10   Michael F. Bryan, "Island Money," *Economic Commentary*, Federal Reserve Bank of Cleveland, February 1, 2004, https://www.clevelandfed.org/publications/economic-commentary/2004/ec-20040201-island-money.

11   For reference, as a gauge of purchasing power, at the time of Augustus, a private in the Roman army earned two hundred to three hundred denarii a year (although after deductions for his food, uniform, funeral expenses, and other costs, his spendable income would have been forty-five to sixty denarii a year).

12   Alan W. Pense, "The Decline and Fall of the Roman Denarius," *Materials Characterization* 29, no. 2 (September 1992): 213–14, https://doi.org/10.1016/1044-5803(92)90116-Y.

Interestingly, the variously sized copper coins in widespread use before the imperial establishment of the denarius were valued by weight measured as fractions of the Roman pound, which weighed 325 grams, the approximate weight of the early British pound, and was called the Libra, the initial name of Facebook's planned digital currency.

Fewer than a hundred years after it was officially standardized, the value of the denarius began to erode, and the infamous Nero was the first emperor to oversee its debasement.[13] In 64 AD, he lowered its weight from 3.9 to 3.41 grams and reduced its silver content to 93.5 percent. In doing so, he established a pattern that would repeat several times during the Roman Empire, plague many subsequent currencies, and inspire (among other issues) the early-twenty-first-century drive to engineer a better one. Figure 1.3 shows how the weight and the silver content were lowered, emperor by emperor, until two hundred years later, the denarius was a copper coin with such a thin veneer of silver paint that it rubbed off shortly after its minting.

---

13 Debasement is the reduction of the silver content of a coin, for example, by reducing its weight or purity.

Fineness of Early Roman Imperial Silver Coins

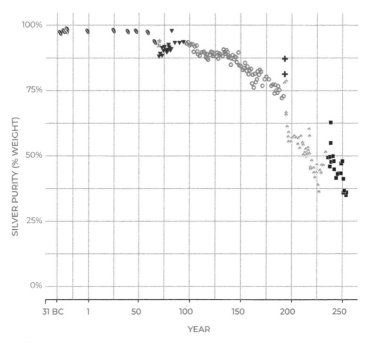

Era

🝐 Julio-Claudians
★ Civil war (AD 69)
▼ Flavians
○ Antonines
✚ Civil war (AD 193)
♠ Severans
■ Third century crisis

Figure 1.3: The decline of the silver content of coins in the Roman Empire (Source: "Fineness of Early Roman Imperial Silver Coins," Nicholas Perrault, III, March 18, 2018, https://commons.wikimedia.org/wiki/File:Fineness_of_early_ Roman_Imperial_silver_coins.png.)

The Arabic dinar takes its name from the denarius and is still used today in several countries.

In those two hundred years, the denarius lost almost all its purchasing power and eventually disappeared despite several attempts to revive it. This devaluation happened more quickly in rural areas than in Rome, with people keeping the older, heavier, and higher-silver-content coins for themselves while continuing to circulate the inferior ones in an early example of Gresham's Law.

Gresham's Law: The monetary principle that "bad money drives out good money" whenever nominally equivalent representations of value become distorted by devaluation, prompting people to hoard the more valuable currency and circulate the less valuable.

1.iv. Cigarette Money

Cigarette money (*Zigarettenwährung*), the last of the commodity-based currencies we'll explore, is interesting primarily because it illustrates money's profound utility. In extreme situations like Nazi Germany, in POW camps and prisons, with no central authority to organize a monetary system, one seems to spontaneously arise. R. A. Radford, writing in 1945, described cigarettes as having attained full currency status, with an ad hoc store selling food, toiletries, and the like for "a fixed price in [Red Cross] cigarettes."[14] Even in communities with little else to unite them, money is simply so useful that it evolves independently.

2. REPRESENTATIVE MONEY

Had cigarettes been so bulky or so fragile that they became difficult to carry around, they might instead have been stored by a few respected members of the community as tobacco was in Colonial America. There, a pound of tobacco had a set amount of purchasing power and warehouse receipts were used as a crude form of representative money. These people might then have issued receipts marked with the number of cigarettes they held for an individual, and those slips, accepted in lieu of cigarettes, could potentially become a currency themselves.[15] Because the receipts represented the cigarettes, this would have been an example of representative money. Representative money is valuable because it can both take the place of and be exchanged for something of intrinsic value, despite having little or no value of its own.

Representative Currency: money that uses some material (usually paper) to represent some form of commodity money (usually coins/precious metals).

---

14   R. A. Radford, "The Economic Organization of a P.O.W. Camp," *Economica* 12, no. 48 (November 1945): 192, https://doi.org/10.2307/2550133.

15   In fact, this is quite close to what actually happened in Colonial America, where a pound of tobacco had a set amount of purchasing power, with warehouse receipts for the tobacco used as a crude form of representative money.

In China, use of representative money dates from 119 BC, when foot-square pieces of brightly decorated, white deerskin were issued by the government to represent certain sums of copper coins.[16] In the West, we can pick up the history of representative money where we left it geographically—in Italy. There, beginning in the fourteenth and continuing through the fifteenth century, an early form of representative currency evolved from what were functionally Medici family IOUs. A person leaving gold or silver with the Medici was given a receipt and, because people trusted the family, they trusted those receipts to such an extent that they became a viable currency. Such representative currencies were the dominant form of money until recently. The US dollar, for example, was representative of the gold for which it could be nominally redeemed until the 1970s.

2.i. Paper Money

In addition to the first representative money, China holds claim to the creation of the first government-backed paper currency, the *jiaozi*.[17] Developed in response to the problem of carrying steadily more iron coins over increasingly long distances as the Song Dynasty (960–1279) expanded, the jiaozi was also the first paper currency to experience the inflation-and-reform cycle that afflicted so many of its successors.

---

16 W. Vissering, *On Chinese Currency: Coin and Paper Money* (Leiden: E. J. Brill, 1877), 38–39.

17 Richard von Glahn, "Re-Examining the Authenticity of Song Paper Money Specimens," *Journal of Song-Yuan Studies* 36 (2006): 80–82, https://www.jstor.org/stable/23496299; Ulrich Theobald, "Jiaozi and Qianyin, Early Paper Money," ChinaKnowledge, May 10, 2016, http://www.chinaknowledge.de/History/Terms/jiaozi.html.

The ubiquity of paper money is largely due to its portability. Simply put, paper money is convenient. It weighs less than coins and takes up less space. One million US dollars weigh only about ten kilos and, as we all know from the movies, can be carried in a single large briefcase. Additionally, because a paper bill is an abstraction, it can represent both very large and very small values dependent only on the numbers printed on it.[18] These advantages are somewhat offset by how easy paper money is to counterfeit. A cowry shell is a cowry shell, and a pound of silver is (or was) worth a pound sterling, but a piece of paper isn't worth anything if it isn't a genuine bill.

2.ii. The British Pound

The cowry shell may be the oldest form of currency, but the British pound is the oldest still in continuous use since its creation. Dating from the eighth century, the pound gets its name from the weight of silver it was originally worth. At the time, a pound's worth of silver was equivalent to 240 silver pennies. Converted to a bimetallic gold/silver standard by Sir Isaac Newton, the pound eventually lost its connection to silver in everything but name.

The pound was the leading world currency in the nineteenth century and remained relatively stable during that time only to lose 99 percent of its purchasing power during the twentieth century. It detached from the gold standard at the beginning of

---

18   Until recently, Singapore produced a 10,000 Singapore dollar note worth over $7,000, and the Bank of England has produced (but does not circulate) 1 million and even 100 million pound notes.

the First World War, relinked briefly in 1925, and was decoupled again in 1931.[19] At the end of the Second World War, under the Bretton Woods System, the pound and many other world currencies were linked to the US dollar, which was at that point still backed by gold.

2.iii. Three New Issues

Because of their many advantages, representative currencies quickly replaced commodity money in most places. But the nature of representative money introduced two significant new issues: the double-spend problem and fractional reserve banking.

The Double-Spend Problem

Once transactions were conducted by exchanging something that represented wealth stored elsewhere, it became possible for people to "spend" that stored value more than once. The most obvious example is check fraud, where a person knowingly writes a check on an account that doesn't hold enough money to cover it.

In a simplified example, if Alice has a hundred dollars in her checking account, she can spend it twice by writing hundred-dollar checks to two different merchants, Bob and Charlie. Since there is only enough money in her account to

---

19 Rothko Research, "A History of the British Pound," *Rothko Research* (blog), January 5, 2017, https://rothkoresearch.com/2017/01/05/a-history-of-the-british-pound/.

honor one of these checks, whichever merchant deposits Alice's check first gets her hundred dollars while the other merchant goes unpaid.

Fractional Reserve Banking

There's a legend designating goldsmiths as the originators of fractional reserve banking, which, while possibly apocryphal, is useful nonetheless. By this account, a wily goldsmith in the practice of holding gold for other merchants to whom he issued receipts realized that he could augment his income by making loans of that stored gold to other people. Because he made (and collected interest on) those loans by issuing additional receipts for gold rather than the actual gold, he could effectively loan the same ounce to one or more people. Being clever, he held some fraction of the merchants' gold in reserve to pay out if someone came to cash in a receipt. But in a very real sense, he was creating something from nothing—a new kind of money.

The new problem that the goldsmith had created, and that could not have been an issue with commodity money, was that there were now more gold receipts in circulation than there was gold in existence. If everyone who trusted the goldsmith to store their gold for them tried to collect it on the same day, there wouldn't be enough to cover the receipts of deposits—the money—he had issued unless he could call in all the loans he had made.

The same processes are used by banks today. Today, banks use a similar technique, which also multiplies the value in circulation compared with the initial deposit.[20] Banks are obliged to hold a reserve in order to satisfy customers' withdrawal demands and are permitted to lend the rest of the deposits they receive. This reserve is typically a small fraction (the so-called "fractional reserve") of total deposits, and for simplicity in the following example is 10 percent (the "fractional reserve rate").

Imagine Alice deposited $100 in her savings account at Big Bank. Big Bank then loaned $90 to Bob. Alice and Bob now have access to $190 between them. Big Bank has effectively created $90 out of nothing. This process is illustrated in Figure 1.4.

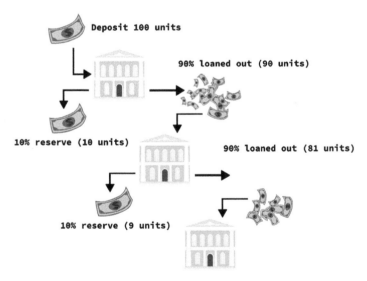

Banks artificially create money in the economy by making loans based on fractional reserve banking. In this example, what started out as 100 units of money deposited becomes 171 units of money loaned.

Figure 1.4: Fractional reserve banking

---

20   With no implication of fraudulent activity or intent.

If Bob then bought $90 worth of goods from Carol, and Carol, in turn, deposited that $90 in her savings account at Big Bank, Big Bank could loan $81 to Dave. This process could continue further, and with a fractional reserve rate of 10 percent, up to $900 could be created by Big Bank in this way. This practice of fractional reserve banking is how commercial banks today create something from nothing—money out of thin air.[21]

The US central bank differentiates between various types of money, of which the two most important are:

- M0—physical currency, i.e., bills and coins

- M1—money commonly used for payment, consisting of: M0 plus bank deposits and checks.

M1 is basically the currency in circulation, which includes the money "created" by commercial banks.

> **Fractional Reserve Banking:** A system of banking where commercial banks hold only a fraction of their depositors' assets and lend the rest, effectively creating money.

Because banks spend their newly created dollars at old-dollar rates, fractional reserve banking transfers wealth to those

---

21   The formula for the maximum total amount of money that can result at the end of this process is (initial deposit)/(fractional reserve rate). For example, an initial deposit of USD 100 could result in a total money supply of USD 1,000 if the fractional reserve rate is 10 percent. This means that on top of the existing USD 100, another USD 900 is created by commercial banks. If the reserve rate is 5 percent, the total money supply could be up to USD 2,000.

closest to the money supply and away from those further from it—away from Bob and Carol to the owners of Big Bank. In another application of Gresham's Law, the owners will spend the new "bad" money before the inflation, which it created, reduces its value. To some, this renders money created through fractional reserve banking less than fully legitimate.

There may be an impression that in this way, money is created from nothing. However, every time money is created through this process, a corresponding liability is also incurred, so that the balance nets to zero, as the new money created is offset by the liability.

Nevertheless, fractional reserve banking is by far the dominant system today, while full reserve banking, under which banks are required to always hold 100 percent of their depositors' assets, is extraordinarily rare. It's very much in banks' interest to keep it this way. Every dollar held in reserve is one less a bank can loan, and the more a bank lends, the more it makes.

Bank Runs

The vast majority of banks use fractional reserve banking. If deteriorating economic or political conditions prompt a significant percentage of depositors to withdraw their money, the inability of a bank to pay their depositors might start a bank run. This happened in Cyprus and Greece during the European debt crisis, with people waiting for days in long lines to reclaim a portion of the money they had deposited. Obviously, the higher a bank's reserves, the more customers it can satisfy, and there are laws that theoretically protect depositors. None of this, however, changes the simple fact that the practice of fractional reserve banking means banks are never in a position to simultaneously honor all their customers' deposits.

A **bank run** (or **run on the banks**) occurs when many customers attempt to withdraw their deposits because they are worried about the bank's solvency. This can drive still more people to withdraw their funds, increasing the probability of default, and can cause a feedback loop in which customers become more anxious and make more withdrawals until the system collapses.

3. FIAT MONEY

Fiat money, which takes its name from the Latin word meaning "let it be done," is one level of abstraction further from something of intrinsic value. In commodity money, the currency itself is a commodity and valuable in its own right. In representative money, the currency represents a commodity and is backed by it. It is valuable because it can be exchanged for the commodity it represents. Fiat money has no relationship to any commodity and is backed by nothing. It is created and made legal tender by government decree (fiat) and derives its value from that decree.[22]

---

22 N. Gregory Mankiw, *Brief Principles of Macroeconomics*, 7th ed. (Stamford: Cengage Learning, 2015), 219–20.

In 1971, toward the end of the Vietnam War, Richard Nixon detached the US dollar from its gold backing, rendering it a fiat currency. Other nations followed suit, with the Swiss, the last significant gold-standard system, going fiat in 1999. Today, no state currency is backed by anything other than the government that issued it.

Once uncoupled, the relative value of gold to the dollar increased dramatically. In 1971, gold was $35 an ounce. Just two years later, it had risen to $120. Today, an ounce of gold sells for $1500, representing a 40-fold devaluation of the dollar relative to gold over the last fifty years.[23]

4. MONEY AND THE STATE

Historically, nation-states have claimed the exclusive right to issue currency. From 118 BC, when the Chinese first issued leather banknotes, through the denarius and the British pound to the present, most conventional currencies have been under direct government control. In fact, the idea of government itself almost depends on the ability to claim and defend a monopoly over two things: money and violence. When a state controls the currency, it's able to create and destroy money to suit its purposes or placate its people. As the interests of the state and the people are not necessarily the same, the government does not always act in the interest of the people. For this reason, since at least the rule of Nero, money under state control often loses its value over time.

---

23 The current gold price can be found at https://goldprice.org/gold-price.html.

4.i. Central Banks

Central banks arose as something like a guild or professional association to facilitate the coordination of multiple private banks issuing multiple currencies and to provide some protection from or distribution of harm, when individual banks got into trouble. The Bank of England was established by Parliament in 1694 as a private bank with special privileges (including the sole right to issue British pounds in exchange for immediately loaning the government a great deal of money). It became the first quasi-governmental entity to take on the responsibilities of a central bank, serving as the country's lender of last resort, loaning funds to financial institutions during the financial crisis of 1866 to forestall a breakdown of the financial system.

Central banks like the Bank of England have some control over the credit supply and the money private banks create through the practice of fractional reserve banking. By lowering the fraction of its assets a bank must hold in reserve, central banks indirectly permit commercial banks to create more money.

When, for example, a central bank lowers the fractional reserve rate from 10 percent to 5 percent, the total potential amount of currency in circulation doubles.[24] Increasing the money supply leads, all else being equal, to the money already in circulation losing its value.[25] This allows the central bank

---

24 This can be determined by the formula (money multiplier) = 1/(reserve requirement).

25 I.e., the velocity of money, which is a measure of how frequently money is transferred between parties in an economy in a given time period.

to operate something of a dial between the amount of money available for banks to loan and the security of the money that they owe their depositors. When the central authorities think too much credit has been created—that people are borrowing too much or that banks have become unstable—they can raise this reserve rate, requiring banks to retain more of their assets, thus creating less credit and making banks more secure. However, central banks mainly use interest rates (instead of the fractional reserve rate) to exert control on the macro-economic environment.

This British model of a state-owned central bank with a monopoly on the issuance of government-debt-backed fiat money, and serving as the lender of last resort to the nation's private banks, was quickly adopted by other nations: the Federal Reserve in the United States, the European Central Bank of the Eurozone, and the Bank of Japan and People's Bank of China in their respective countries. Today, these national central banks have a central bank of their own, the International Monetary Fund (IMF), which performs many of the same functions. It coordinates between national financial systems and steps in when a country and its central bank are in trouble and need external help.

4.ii. Private Money

Currency is not inherently government issued. In the US, for example, between 1837 and 1866, the federal government put no regulations on who was entitled to issue currencies. Private entities—from individual states and municipalities to churches, banks, and railroad companies—all devised, printed, and circulated their own money with such enthusiasm that, by 1863, there were eight thousand different currencies in use.[26]

Today, perhaps the closest things to private money in the US and EU are airline frequent flier miles, although technically, there's no reason why an oil and gas company like Exxon couldn't issue "Exxon dollars." In fact, if those dollars could be redeemed for tanks of gas the way airline miles can be for plane tickets, Exxon dollars would have something more tangible backing them than the dollar does.

Private money, when legal, still presents challenges. If the issuing business entity fails or goes bankrupt, the currency can lose some or all of its value. While the same is true of government-backed money, states typically have longer life spans than corporations. As a result, at present, we have a very monolithic, worldwide financial system of central banks, fiat currencies, and private institutions that keep only a small percentage of their investors' deposits in reserve. Today, there are very few other options, but this hasn't always been the case.

4.iii. Free Banking

Historically, several countries' economies have operated without a central bank either as a lender of last resort or the monopoly issuer of currency. In eighteenth and nineteenth century Scotland, for example, a system of competitive banking replaced the central bank. Major banks issued their own

---

26   Rema Oxandaboure, "5 Things You May Not Know about Money," *ECONCEPTS* (blog), San Francisco Fed Economic Education Group, June 11, 2014, https://econcepts.edublogs.org/2014/06/11/5-things-you-may-not-know-about-money/.

notes and accepted one another's. If banknotes issued by one bank were deposited at another bank, they would be accepted by that bank, and would be returned via a clearing mechanism to the original bank. In this way, a bank could not over-issue banknotes in the hope that they would be deposited at other banks that would then cover the gold or silver owed to the depositor. This practice incentivized cautious decision-making and reduced the chances that one institution could damage the stability of any other. A policy that assigned unlimited liability to bank shareholders also encouraged responsible stewardship. Bankers, not banks—the individuals and not the institution—jointly but personally guaranteed all debts their bank incurred. It's interesting to think how differently bankers today might behave were that still the case.

In fact, a system where financial institutions compete with one another, issuing their own notes on their own terms and arranging for systemic protection among themselves without government involvement, has advocates, among them, Nobel prize–winning economist Friedrich Hayek.[27] Hayek has argued such a free-banking system would liberate not only banks but their customers. Financial institutions, he asserts, would be less vulnerable to political pressure and driven by consumer demand to maintain price stability by holding a larger percentage of their resources in reserve.

This, of course, assumes a state willing to cede its monopoly on the issuance of money and is not without some risk. Hayek's detractors are quick to point out that, without a central bank

---

27   F. A. Hayek, *Denationalisation of Money: The Argument Refined* (London: The Institute of Economic Affairs, 1976).

operating as a backstop, there would be nothing to keep a failing bank from going under and taking all its customers' wealth with it.

CHAPTER SUMMARY

We interact with money so regularly that it can become something on which we depend without understanding what it is and how it works. It's easy to forget that, while money has always been an abstraction, it's such an incredibly useful one that in those extraordinary times when one currency breaks down, another seems to arise almost spontaneously to take its place.

As different as shells and cigarettes, carved stones and Roman coins are, they all still illustrate the fundamentally abstract nature of money. Even though these representative examples of commodity money all had some intrinsic value independent of their use as currency, they each allowed for only a fairly limited range of transactions. Commodity money must be physically present to be exchanged.

Representative money solved this issue while introducing new ones—the double-spend problem and fractional reserve banking with its risk of bank runs. Fiat currencies and the rise of central banks, while doing little to address the issues introduced by representative currencies, gave the governments that issue and regulate them more control over the amount of money and debt available.

From the cowry shell to today's fiat currencies and central banks, money has looked and behaved differently throughout its long evolution, but it has fulfilled many of the same functions from its beginning to the present day. To compare the relative strengths and weaknesses of such a diverse field and to consider how the next stage of money's evolution might improve upon its history, it's useful to articulate those functions money needs to perform and to create a list of traits by which currencies can be more objectively compared. As we will see later, bitcoin, the original cryptocurrency, has several well-designed traits that would make it an excellent form of money.

2

THE FUNCTIONS AND PROPERTIES OF MONEY

WE HADN'T THOUGHT MUCH ABOUT WHAT MONEY IS AND HOW it works until we found ourselves grappling with the idea of an invented internet currency. If money had no physical form, was it money? We'd never used coins or bills to buy a car or pay rent. We knew that international currencies were no longer backed by precious metals, so what gave them value? And credit cards? If they aren't currency but rather act like it, what are they?

These questions about one of the most integral parts of our everyday lives are interesting in and of themselves. In light of a digital currency, they became even more so. Learning competing philosophies of money, the differences between a currency and a payment system, and the functions and traits that qualify both snail shells and cigarettes as money deepened our understanding of and fluency with money. Ultimately the questions and answers expanded our thinking about what makes a good currency, how we might compare one with another, and what a better one might be.

Note on terminology: in this book we use the terms "money" and "currency" interchangeably. Other sources make differentiations between the two, but we do not think that insisting on this would add to the clarity or detract from the accuracy of this book.

1. THREE FUNCTIONS OF MONEY

Why is a cigarette in a POW camp a currency while one from the quickie mart isn't?[28] A cigarette, a shell, or a piece of paper needs to fulfill three functions to qualify as a good form of money: it needs to operate as a medium of exchange, a unit of account, and a store of value.[29] Some currencies fulfill all these criteria, others do not.

1.i. A Medium of Exchange

Without money, every transaction must involve a "coincidence of wants," where both parties have and are willing to exchange a good or service the other requires but does not have. If Alice wants some apples but only has potatoes, and Bob has apples, but could use a nice cheese, their wants (Alice's for apples, Bob's for cheese) don't coincide. They can only do business if their needs coincide. A direct trade would only work if Alice wants apples and Bob wants potatoes. Therefore, for this system to work, a coincidence of wants has to occur—a precondition that will in all probability in most cases not occur.

---

28   Unless the quickie mart cigarette landed in a POW camp!

29   Irena Asmundson and Ceyda Oner, "What Is Money?," *Finance and Development* 49, no. 3 (September 2012): 52, https://www.imf.org/external/pubs/ft/fandd/2012/09/basics.htm.

This is obviously inefficient, puts constraints on trade, and limits economic output. The system works better when everyone agrees on something that they'll all accept in trade for anything of value. Debby trades a cigarette for Eliza's apples because Eliza knows someone else will take the cigarette in payment for his cheese. Even though Eliza doesn't smoke, the cigarette loses none of its value because it operates as the agreed-upon object of universal trade—the medium of exchange.

Medium of Exchange: an intermediary instrument, which may not necessarily be useful for the person possessing it, used to facilitate trade by serving as an agreed-upon standard of value.

1.ii. A Unit of Account

Sometimes also called "measure of value," money's unit-of-account function is a logical extension of the medium of exchange. Because money is the common denominator in all the exchanges, Bob can know how many potatoes an apple is worth. Money establishes the relative value of goods both one to the other and across location and time. An apple in the city is worth more than it is on the farm and less in late summer when it's in season than in winter when it's had to be preserved.

Money's ability to measure value also unifies an economy that would otherwise be divided by disjointed units of account. Nobody would measure the value of a farm in apples. Should Debby decide to buy the whole orchard, without money, the asking price might be in horses. With houses measured in horses and apples in cheese, it'd be very complicated to accurately assess the price of the orchard. Having a unit of account allows consistent and coherent pricing of goods on both ends of the price spectrum. It's the only way participants in a market can maintain an account of how much purchasing power they possess.

> **Unit of Account:** the trait that allows money to account for and compare the value of different goods and services. Also called "Measure of Value."

1.iii. A Store of Value

Because money allows people to abstract value from trade goods and to conduct all their transactions in a common currency, it encapsulates value (which doesn't necessarily mean it can hold onto it). A currency carries out its third function as a store of value when it holds that value and allows trade over time or space. Long-term contracts are impossible otherwise. If Eliza wants to sell her orchard for more than Debby has, she will only agree to accept the balance in the future if she believes the money she gets later will represent the same relative purchasing power it has today.

> **Store of Value:** the ability to purchase with the same sum of money at least the same or equivalent goods and services.

2. TRAITS OF MONEY

To fulfill its functions, money must have certain traits.[30] Apples would have trouble storing value because they rot. Horses are a poor medium of exchange because they can't be spent incrementally, say one-sixteenth of a horse for a dozen apples. Nor do they fit nicely in pockets.

2.i. Scarcity

There's a reason money doesn't grow on trees. More specifically, there's a reason leaves would make terrible money. Who would trade his horse or even her apple for a leaf? Economies and trade are, at the most fundamental level, about managing scarce resources. Because money is used to represent the value of these resources, money itself must be scarce.

Initially, this was accomplished by using things that were physically scarce like a very particular kind of shell or precious metal. Remember, rai stones weren't fashioned from local stone. Representative money derived its value from the physical scarcity of the gold or silver by which it was backed. When a currency decouples from precious metals (and becomes a fiat currency), only a central bank can issue a currency with no physical backing and still retain enough credibility to continue to be used.

---

30   W. Stanley Jevons, *Money and the Mechanism of Exchange* (New York: D. Appleton and Company, 1877), 31.

Scarcity could be impacted by its security. Money that is easy to counterfeit will not be able to maintain its scarcity. Money that is easily counterfeited becomes much less scarce very quickly. Coins are vulnerable to counterfeiting since it can be very difficult without measuring equipment to tell the difference between one made almost entirely of precious metal and one merely painted or plated with it.

The Superdollar

Beginning in the 1980s, extremely high-quality counterfeit US hundred dollar bills entered circulation, posing a significant enough threat to the economy that they prompted the introduction of the 3D security ribbon as well as aggressive international forensic action. While the origin of these realistic fakes was never determined, the US government accused North Korea of being responsible.

2.ii. Durability

To perform the function of storing value, a currency needs to be durable—not subject to decay and difficult to damage. Denarii first used two thousand years ago are still recognizable, even readable, today, and cowries—small and involuted—are among the sturdiest of shells. As a counterexample, eggs, which are easily damaged and do not remain fresh for long, would be a poor currency as they are not durable.

2.iii. Portability

Durability is obviously a contributing factor to portability, as a fragile currency would risk breakage in transport, but weight and bulk are also factors. The ideal is a sturdy medium with the capacity to compress maximum value into a minimum of mass, which is why precious metals like gold or silver have been often used historically as forms of money. Paper money has a clear portability advantage over heavy coins and even heavier rai stones and over cowry shells and cigarettes, which, while relatively lightweight, take up quite a lot of space.

2.iv. Divisibility

Divisibility enhances a currency's ability to function as both a medium of exchange and unit of account. It's what allows a person who sells an orchard to use their proceeds from a high-value sale to pay for a series of low-value purchases, and a person to collect their profits on multiple small sales to buy a more expensive item. The utility of this trait explains why the individual unit of most currencies—the single cigarette or penny coin—is usually of relatively little value but can be easily bundled into denominated coins and boxes of cigarettes. Cowry shells, likewise low-value, were sufficiently uniform in size that they could be traded by weight. Gold bars, on the other hand, were not easily divisible.

2.v. Fungibility

Fungibility, perhaps the least obvious and intuitive of the traits of money, is the one that enables a unit of a currency to be interchangeable with any other of the same denomination. Gemstones provide an excellent counterexample. Rubies, like gold, are scarce, durable, and portable, but one gram of gold is, for practical purposes, virtually indistinguishable from any other, while no two one-gram rubies are exactly the same. A gram of gold in the shape of a square is worth as much as a round gram, but two rubies of the same shape and weight will differ in value depending on their clarity and color.

Gold is fungible and rubies aren't, but that doesn't necessarily mean gold coins are. Coins that derive their value from their precious metal content are subject to wear, damage, and tampering and to changing manufacturing standards. One cowry shell, in contrast, is worth the same as any other. Likewise, paper money, having no inherent value, is fungible, but rai stones, with their worth derived in part from their history, are not.

Transactions conducted in fungible currencies move more quickly because the value of each unit doesn't need to be assessed individually. Therefore, the more fungible a currency is, the better it can perform its functions as a unit of account and a medium of exchange.

2.vi. Security and Counterfeiting

A money form that is intended to act as a medium of exchange is conditional on its broad acceptance amongst market participants. This depends on those using the money being able to trust that it is genuine. Resistance to counterfeiting is important in establishing this confidence. Large quantities of counterfeit money will tend to devalue the currency on a macro level, and for this reason counterfeiting has also been used as a weapon in war, with belligerents trying to destabilize the economy of the opponent by introducing large quantities of false currency.

Banknotes, as a printed form of money, are a clear target for counterfeiters, but modern notes have many features that make it difficult to create convincing false notes, such as holographic images, foil components, transparent features, micro letters, and raised ink. Ultraviolet lights, detector pens, and banknote testing machines can help to check whether banknotes are genuine or not.

Coins attract counterfeiters who can attempt to use a less valuable metal than the genuine coin, such as tungsten instead of gold. Making counterfeit coins by plating a less valuable metal with the precious metal so it appears genuine is a prac-tice dating back thousands of years.

Digital forms of currency are held in deposit by banks, which are regulated by authorities, and the ability to counterfeit money held by a bank in this form is effectively non-existent.

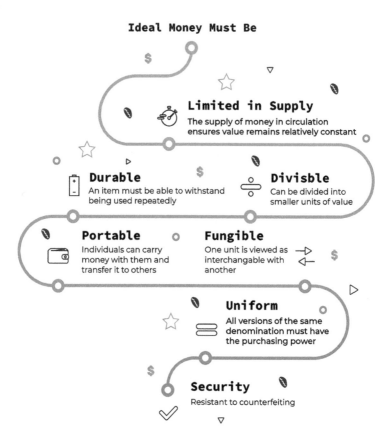

Figure 2.1: Traits of money (Source: W. Stanley Jevons, Money and the Mechanism of Exchange [New York: D. Appleton and Company, 1877], 30-40.)

3. ASSESSING MONEY BY FUNCTIONS AND TRAITS

With these three functions and six traits of currencies established, it becomes possible to evaluate and compare currencies, including cryptocurrencies, against a common set of metrics.

3.i. Cowry Shells

Cowry shells performed all three functions remarkably well. They were a widely accepted medium of exchange and a unit of account that allowed the value of dissimilar items to be measured. They were a good store of value because they were both durable and portable. They were intrinsically valuable because they were scarce, and uniform enough to be fungible and to allow for assessment by weight. This allowed them to be divisible down to the single shell. Little wonder they were in use for almost four thousand years.

3.ii. Rai Stones

Used primarily for high-value purchases, rai stones were certainly a good store of value but only to a limited extent a good medium of exchange.[31] They were not fungible, and for that reason not a good unit of account. Because they were difficult to carve from non-native stone, they were both scarce and durable. But they were neither portable nor fungible.

3.iii. Roman Denarii

The denarius (and most other precious-metal coins) was a state-issued medium of exchange that was an excellent unit of account but an imperfect store of value subject to both

---

31 Systems of reciprocity largely managed the exchange of lower-value items on the island.

debasement and inflation.[32] Throughout history, royal, imperial, and elected state authorities in charge of issuing and controlling money have made decisions with long-term consequences to solve short-term problems. Issuing more representative currency or lowering the precious metal content of commodity currency, for example, to fund a war, or as a response to a crisis situation or economic depression, gradually decreases the purchasing power of a nation's currency.

The denarius in particular and coins fashioned of precious metals in general derive their scarcity from that of gold and silver, and they're durable, divisible, and portable, but less fungible than even the humble cowry shell, and easier to counterfeit.[33]

3.iv. Cigarette Money

Of the currencies we've chosen as examples, cigarettes satisfy the fewest of money's functions and possess fewer of its desirable traits. They are, however, an excellent example of the kind of commodity that gets pressed into service as a currency when other forms of money are not available or are widely distrusted. They served as a medium of exchange allowing for the indirect exchange of goods, and they provided a single point of reference for the pricing of other goods and services. They were not, however, a great store of value. Since prisoners typically didn't need to draw up long-term contracts and weren't able to travel great distances, this was less of an issue.

---

32 While debasement refers to the reduction of the silver content of a coin, inflation means the decline of a coin's purchasing power.

33 Different silver coins from different periods would not have the same silver content so would not be interchangeable in value, or fungible.

In war, captured enemy soldiers, known as "prisoners of war" (POW), were interned in purpose-built camps until the conflict ended. The Red Cross by convention provided them with various supplies for daily life, including cigarettes. Rationed and provided by the Red Cross to inmates, cigarettes were scarce, and, although they could be stolen, they were fairly secure against forgery. They weren't durable, but boxes of them were easily divisible, even if an individual cigarette was not. Lightweight enough to be carried in the small quantities most people had, they weren't particularly portable since they could not be easily compressed. They were, however, fungible. Since there wasn't access to different brands or qualities, one Red Cross cigarette was interchangeable with any other.

3.v. Representative and Fiat Money

Representative money, typically backed by precious metal and by the state, had a great deal of overlap with the denarius. An outstanding unit of account and medium of exchange, representative money was only as good a store of value as the precious metal for which it could be exchanged. Representative money's scarcity derived from making it difficult to counterfeit and the underlying scarcity of the commodity that it represented. Representative money, however, was usually much more portable, divisible, and fungible than most commodity money, making it significantly easier to use. It also enabled the transfer of value by written (and later by digital) order.

Fiat money, as a direct descendent of representative currency, kept much the same profile with one significant difference. Since it can be produced at will, it utterly fails the scarcity test, making it a less reliable store of value.

3.vi. Comparison of Different Currencies

In the following table we summarize our assessment for various currencies with regard to the traits that we have discussed in this section, our scale ranging from "--" for "very poor" to "++" for "very good." Certainly our judgments are subjective and debatable, but the general pros and cons of the currencies are apparent, and that they often differ quite significantly from one another.

	Cowry Shells	Rai Stones	Gold	Diamonds	Fiat
Durable	+	+	++	++	++
Portable	0	--	+	+	+
Fungible	+	--	+	--	+
Verifiable (Resistance to counterfeiting)	+	++	0	-	-
Divisible	+	--	0	-	+
Scarcity	+	+/-	+	++	-

Figure 2.2: Comparison of the traits of cowry shells, rai stones, gold, diamonds, and fiat money

4. PAYMENT SYSTEMS

A system that facilitates the transfer of monetary value from one party to another is called a "payment system."

Payment system: a method of transferring monetary value, including the necessary people, technology, and standards.

Transaction: the transfer of monetary value.

Payment systems can be evaluated by three significant attributes:

- Security,

- Convenience,

- Mediation.

Security is a measure of how difficult it is to create illegitimate transfers of value through theft, counterfeit, or fraud. **Convenience** is how easy it is to use the payment system.

Mediation refers to whether transactions require the involvement of a third party or can be carried out directly between market participants, in what's known as peer-to-peer transactions. These attributes are interrelated, e.g., often improving security makes the system harder to use. It is helpful to understand when a change in one attribute affects the others.

Peer-to-peer transactions: transactions done directly, one person to another (without intermediary), e.g., US dollar cash transactions.

The US dollar uses different payment systems, each of which has its own strengths and weaknesses. The physical transfer of cash, while good for small, local transactions, is subject to theft. Paper checks, which transfer value by order, are more secure than cash, but they can be forged or stolen, and they're impractical for making purchases, as many stores no longer accept them. Transactions by check can still be conducted face-to-face, but they continue to be mediated by a bank. Wiring dollars is yet more secure, but international transfers are often expensive and slower than those made within the US.

Electronic systems are more secure and convenient for most transactions. Credit cards, while certainly more secure than cash, are still subject to fraud. The customer is insured against this, but the security checks banks put in place to protect themselves occasionally result in legitimate charges being declined. Likewise, PayPal is quite secure and, once set up, convenient for most online purchases.[34]

---

34   PayPal is a centralized solution and can suspend your account if there is a dispute.

Payment system	Security	Convenience	Mediation
Physical Settlement	Cash can easily be stolen; Difficult to prove transaction took place without receipt	Good for local transactions on smaller scale; otherwise often impractical	Peer-to-peer
Bank Wire	Good	Good within currency zone; can be slow and expensive for international wires	Via commercial bank
Credit Card	Good, however, credit card fraud exists (against which consumer is insured)	Good (fast), however, security checks can lead to card payments being rejected in non-standard cases (e.g travelling abroad)	Via credit card processor and commerical bank
Check	Medium	Medium, sending and depositing checks require a few steps (e.g visiting a bank)	Via commerical bank
PayPal	Good	Easy once set up	Paypal, financial service provider online, commercial bank

Figure 2.3: Comparison of payment systems

CHAPTER SUMMARY

As we saw in Chapter 1, money appears almost universally in human societies above hunter-gatherer level. The reason why practically every human society invents some kind of money is that money fulfills certain fundamental needs, of which the most significant are found in its three primary functions: store of value, medium of exchange, and unit of account. Currencies can be distinguished by several traits, which determine how well they can perform these functions.

Identifying those traits allows for comparison of currencies, and each of the ones we've studied thus far earned mixed reviews. As money evolved, it often improved on some traits while carrying old issues forward—or even introducing new ones. As we'll see, that trend continues as money moves beyond the physical realm and into the digital one. Now that we have a deeper understanding of what money is and how it works, we'll circle back to its history and track the rise of digital currency through the development of the earliest cryptocurrencies, of which bitcoin was the first.

3

THE DIGITALIZATION
OF MONEY

MONEY, BY DEFINITION, IS AN ABSTRACTION. EVEN SOME-
thing as concrete as a snail shell, when used as currency,
becomes a symbolic representation of value. Money can function as a unit of account exactly because it gives people a way to
measure what things are worth against a common, intangible
standard. The price (the number of shells, coins, or cigarettes)
a person is willing to exchange for an item both determines
and reflects its value.

Shifting from commodity currency to representative currency
requires another layer of abstraction. Now the bill represents
the commodity (usually precious metal) that represents the
value. A horse that is worth a gold coin is purchased with a
note that the former horse owner can exchange either for
a gold coin or for a plus-one addition to the number of gold
coins in his bank's ledger. At this level of abstraction removed
from physical manifestation, the idea of money becomes most
closely connected to a number, for example a bank balance.

This allows the same dollar to be in multiple places at the same time through the practice of fractional reserve banking.

Money Supply 1975-2022

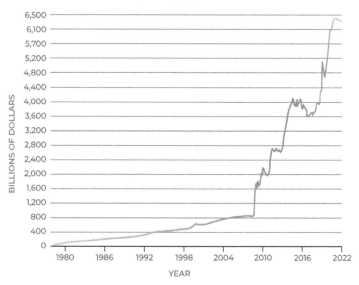

Figure 3.1: The US money supply (Board of Governors of the Federal Reserve System [US], M2, Federal Reserve Bank of St. Louis; data can be found at https://fred.stlouisfed.org/series/M2SL).

When those numbers cease to be ink on a page and become holes in a punched card or a string of ones and zeroes, the abstraction of a symbol of a representation has become so obscure as to be practically impenetrable. We paused our study of the history of money in Chapter 1 before money hit this inflection point to define it by its functions and traits, and then illustrated those traits and functions with currencies belonging to the first two levels of abstraction. Now, with a more secure grounding in what money is, it's time to take that final step.

As we discussed in Chapter 2, a functioning money system needs both units of value and a method (or methods) of transferring those units between people. Digital technology entered the money system as a payment system first.

1. DIGITAL PAYMENT SYSTEMS

The first time a financial transaction was carried out digitally, money was still backed by precious metals. In much the same way that technological advances in the production of paper and printing had quickly been employed to improve money's portability, the introduction of the telegraph in the late 1830s allowed for value to be transferred quickly over long distances.

The telegraph, capitalizing on advances in our understanding of electricity, radically increased the speed and efficiency of communication. Previously the domain of signal fires and semaphores, nearly real-time reliable communication over steadily increasing distances expanded throughout the 1840s as metal wire was spooled out across continents (and eventually oceans). By the 1870s, a young man headed west in the Black Hills Gold Rush could have had money to purchase his shovels and sifting pans wired to him from his father in New York.

While the telegraph made it possible to transfer money digitally (albeit in dots and dashes not ones and zeroes), the money itself was not digital. Only the payment system, the method of transmission, had changed. The actual financial transactions continued to be carried out on paper. The indulgent father from our story, who once might have sent his "Pay to the order of" instructions on a paper check, could now do so in the electromagnetic stops and starts of Morse code, while on either end, bankers with paper ledgers would conduct the actual transaction.

At roughly the same time, the speed at which such transactions could be tabulated was also increasing. Since the abacus, people have used mechanical devices to boost their computational abilities, and, by the end of the nineteenth century, increasingly sophisticated calculating and tabulating machines were improving the speed at which data could be recorded and processed. Banks were quick to adopt this evolving technology for bookkeeping, replacing human, manual, paper-based systems with less expensive, more accurate, faster machines.

In 1955, Bank of America gained a significant competitive advantage by moving from an electromechanical method of administering bank accounts and check-handling systems to an electronic one using magnetic ink.[35] This advance allowed machines to "read" checks, increasing both the number of checks the bank could process and the speed at which it could do so.

With magnetic ink able to store data on paper checks, and with magnetic tapes used for storage, money was poised to become even more portable. Attaching a magnetic strip to a small, plastic card enabled a machine to perform all the steps required to cash a check except the actual dispensing of bills. By the

---

35   SRI International, "75 Years of Innovation: Banking Automation ERMA," The Dish (blog), Medium, February 10, 2021, https://medium.com/dish/75-years-of-innovation-banking-automation-erma-f297ad8c55fd.

late 1960s, that problem had been solved, and automatic teller machines (ATMs) rapidly replaced human bank tellers. ATMs let customers first withdraw and later deposit cash at a wider range of more convenient locations and at more flexible hours than banks had been able to provide.

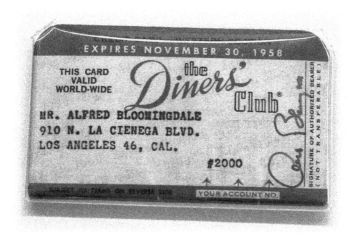

Figure 3.2: An early credit card

As the same technology moved into the retail world, it also made improvements to another of money's key traits—security. Retailers were already using credit cards, but the addition of magnetic strips enabled point-of-sale devices to authenticate transactions more quickly and reduce fraud significantly.

2. DIGITAL FIAT CURRENCIES

The first digital currencies were simply digital versions of existing fiat ones—people had digital dollars in their bank balances, which they could easily convert to paper dollars at an ATM. Currencies' digitization made them easier to use as a medium of exchange, as it enabled money to be transferred more quickly over longer distances. However, the shift to a digital representation made no change in how an established currency fulfilled its function as a unit of account.

Digital versions of fiat currencies also satisfy the tests of other traits. Durability isn't an issue, provided the digital substrates on which they exist are sturdy, and they are, at minimum, as divisible as the underlying fiat currency and potentially more so.

As mentioned above, digital currencies represent a great stride in portability. Physically, you need only a credit card. Electronically, digital money can be sent and "carried" almost anywhere in the world in any amount and practically instantly, at least in theory. In practice, digital money is easier for governments and regulatory agencies to track. For certain amounts and locations, money is still more portable as bills in a suitcase.

Theoretically, digital currencies have perfect fungibility, as they are just represented as ones and zeros. But although one unit of currency is indistinguishable from another, their history is not, and thus people will avoid dealing with money from potentially illegal sources, which means that digital currencies are not perfectly fungible either.

Today, most money is digital—it exists only in computer systems of financial service providers and banks. With $15.3 trillion in the US economy, there was only $1.7 trillion worth of coins and bills as of November 2019.[36] In other words, only about 10 percent of US money exists in physical form. Additionally, 98 percent of financial transactions are carried out digitally today. In Sweden, which has set a goal of becoming entirely cashless by 2023, that percentage is even higher: there, the amount of cash in circulation represents less than 1 percent of the GNP (Gross National Product), and merchants are not required to accept cash as payment.

In 2012 a consortium of six Swedish banks developed Swish, a cashless instant payment app, and, with debit cards issued to anyone older than seven, use of cash there fell by about 50 percent in less than a decade. There are strong incentives for any government to move toward a cashless economy. Because digital transactions are so much easier to monitor and trace than cash payments, tax avoidance becomes much more difficult and black markets are more likely to dry up.

Additionally, a series of extraordinary circumstances created an additional incentive for Sweden to switch from physical cash to digital payments, among them a rather spectacular robbery. In 2009, thieves landed a stolen helicopter on the roof of a cash depot in Västberga. From there, they used explosives to blast their way into the building and made off with 39 million Swedish krona (approximately US$5.5 million) in bills as the police watched helplessly, their own helicopters grounded by what turned out to be a fake bomb planted in their hangar.

---

36 Referring to the money supply, M2, which comprises, inter alia, cash, checking deposits, saving accounts, money market accounts, and money market funds. Board of Governors of the Federal Reserve System, "Money Stock and Debt Measures—H.6 Release," Federal Reserve statistical release, December 12, 2019,

https://www.federalreserve.gov/releases/h6/20191212/.

3. DIGITAL PRIVATE CURRENCIES

Beginning in the 1990s, several innovative people were experimenting with creating new currencies that were digital from the outset. While many early digital currencies ran into operational or governmental obstacles, bitcoin developed and expanded on ideas that had their beginnings here.

3.i. E-Gold

In 1996, two Americans, oncologist Douglas Jackson and lawyer Barry Downey, set up a digital currency backed not by fiat money, but by gold (or other precious metals). Account holders, who eventually numbered in the millions, bought and traded holdings of gold in increments as small as 1/10,000 of a gram, paying by wire transfer or credit card. E-Gold's extraordinary divisibility allowed users to make and receive micropayments—transfers of such minute amounts that they could be sent as a nod of thanks for a blog post or as a gratuity on a larger purchase.

Initially quite lax in the verification of its customers' identities, E-Gold was readily adopted by the unscrupulous, who used it to pay for illegal purchases or to launder illegitimately acquired funds. Even though the company gradually increased its oversight and proactively sought to work with government regulators and law enforcement agencies, even contributing to the apprehension of criminals using its network, it was unable to survive an increasingly harsh regulatory environment.

The US prosecuted E-Gold for unauthorized money transmission. In part because E-Gold had only one database where each participant's holdings were recorded and a single storage facility where the currency's backing precious metal was housed, the government could shut it down completely. The three directors of the company pleaded guilty to operating an unlicensed money transmitting business and engaging in money laundering. They received relatively mild sentences and closed the company. Refunds were paid to account holders after validating their identities.

3.ii. Liberty Dollar

Like E-Gold, the Liberty Dollar was a precious-metal-backed private currency created in the 1990s by an American, Bernard von NotHaus. Having noticed that government-backed currencies tended to lose their value over time, von NotHaus was interested in creating a form of money that might better fulfill a currency's function as a store of value. Pricing the Liberty Dollar at one US dollar, he issued silver coins and paper bills as receipts that could be exchanged for precious metals (predominantly silver) with the express intention of creating a currency that would hold its value and retain its purchasing power over time. And he was successful.

As time proceeded, and the value of silver increased with respect to the US dollar, the Liberty Dollar, which was backed by silver holdings, became worth significantly more as measured by its value in US dollars. For this reason, it was decided to rebase the Liberty Dollar on November 24, 2005, to take this increase in its value into account. In other words, had Alice purchased five Liberty Dollars for five US dollars (a dollar apiece) before November 24, the next day, she would have found ten Liberty Dollars, worth ten US dollars, in her account—very tangible proof that they were holding their value. Although von NotHaus had deliberately designed his coins and bills not to resemble US currency, and although (or perhaps because) the Liberty Dollar was, at the time, the second-biggest currency in the US, the government accused him of counterfeiting, seized his precious metal holdings, and closed down his operation.

3.iii. Linden Dollar

Occupying an interesting middle ground between digital currencies backed by precious metals and the purely virtual currencies that preceded bitcoin, the Linden dollar operates in the virtual world of *Second Life* essentially the same way a fiat currency does in the real world. *Second Life*, designed to be a virtual world in which people carry out all the normal activities of life, boasted almost a million participants at the height of its popularity in the mid-2000s.

Because doing things like stocking a shop or buying a house is integral to gameplay, from its outset, *Second Life* has its own game economy with the Linden dollar as its unit of currency. Participants earn Linden dollars within the game by selling goods or services or purchasing them in real-world fiat currencies. With an exchange rate of a fraction of a cent, the Linden dollar was never intended to be a viable currency beyond the world of *Second Life*, which may account for its survival. Interestingly, one of the earliest exchanges to buy and sell bitcoin was a Linden dollar exchange VirWoX, which expanded into bitcoin trading in April 2011.

3.iv. DigiCash

Founded by American cryptographer David Chaum, DigiCash was the first digital cash system on the internet. It pioneered the use of cryptographic signatures to verify transactions and even managed to establish trial partnerships with a few conventional banks. Users downloaded software and purchased Digi-Cash with fiat currencies, which they could then use to make online purchases. While the system did attract some users—both vendors and merchants—ultimately too few enrolled, and it fell victim to what Chaum called the "chicken/egg problem." Too few customers wanted to make purchases with DigiCash to motivate merchants to try it out, and too few merchants accepted it to motivate customers to use it.

3.v. B-Money

B-Money, like DigiCash, was purely virtual and not backed by gold or other precious metals, but it did not advance beyond a set of documents written in the 1990s by computer engineer Wei Dai. Dai outlined an electronic money system that prefig-ured bitcoin in its proposed digital ledger maintained on non-centralized computers, where a public record of all trans-actions was kept. B-Money was also the first virtual currency to link money generation to the use of computational power to solve mathematical problems, another feature bitcoin would later share.

3.vi. Bitgold

Of the early all-digital currencies, Bitgold—another theoretical currency that, like B-Money, was never actually implemented—came closest to bitcoin. In fact, Satoshi described his creation as an implementation of Bitgold. Created by Nick Szabo, a computer scientist and lawyer who pioneered the "smart" or algorithmic contract, Bitgold also used cryptographic functions.

Szabo was interested in how a digital currency might also be a non-fiat one. The Liberty Dollar and E-Gold used precious metals to sidestep the question, but they were not truly digital and had to be stored and secured in the "real" world. With Bitgold, Szabo set out to create a digital currency backed by a digital form of gold and designed, like real gold, to be scarce and require a great deal of work to mine. Recognizing that computational power was likely to increase, which would make a digital currency progressively easier to create, thus driving inflation, Szabo included timestamping on the premise that the value of any individual unit of Bitgold would be tied to the time it was created. Like rai stones carved before the introduction of iron tools, Bitgold mined when computational power was lower would be worth more, sacrificing fungibility for protection against inflation.

3.vii. Hashcash

Hashcash was first put forward in 1997 as an anti-spam measure by Adam Back, a British cryptographer who would subsequently become CEO of Blockstream, a company active in the ongoing development of bitcoin's core code. Not properly a currency, it was a replacement for DigiCash with the advantage of not requiring users to buy DigiCash. It was a purely code-based solution that allowed a fee to be imposed for the sending of email.

Spam had been an issue for legitimate users of email almost since its inception, capitalizing on the ease and low cost of reproducing information electronically. In the days of paper mail, companies made at least some attempt to qualify their mailing lists to avoid wasting money on the printing and postage of material that would go unread. With the advent of email, not only did mailing costs drop to nearly zero, but it became more expensive to qualify a contact than to send unsolicited offers to huge mailing lists.

At its simplest, Back's solution engineered a cost into the sending of email. For legitimate users, this fee would be vanishingly small, but for spammers sending millions of emails it would be, if not prohibitive, at least a deterrent. Hashcash implemented this fee for email by requiring senders to perform a particular kind of computation called a hash.

We'll explore hash functions in-depth in Chapter 7, but here it's enough to know that their calculation and verification are out of proportion to one another. Calculating a hash is complex enough to require the expenditure of a certain amount of computational power, while verifying that the hash is correct requires almost none. The sender of an email incurs this computational burden while it costs the receiver practically nothing to check that the work has been done. Although this system never gained widespread popularity as applied to email, this concept of a proof of computational work later became an important element of bitcoin.

4. CRYPTOCURRENCIES AND BITCOIN

The word "cryptocurrency" comes from attaching the first half of "cryptography" to the word "currency." Cryptography is itself a portmanteau derived from Greek words *kryptos* (meaning "hidden" or "secret") and *graphein* ("writing"). Here, we'll define cryptocurrency as a digital currency that uses strong cryptography and a decentralized control system. Bitcoin was the first cryptocurrency.

> **Cryptocurrency:** a digital currency that uses strong cryptography and a decentralized control system.

Bitcoin was first proposed by Satoshi Nakamoto in a white paper published to a cryptography mailing list in 2008. The bitcoin network came into being at the start of 2009 when the genesis block (the first block of a blockchain) was defined and generated. We will be looking at what bitcoin is and does in the next chapter.

CHAPTER SUMMARY

The advent of digital technology changed many aspects of money beginning with payment systems, but quickly spread to currency such that today, over 90 percent of US money exists in no other form. As digital money evolved, it also began to be invented. Early pioneers experimented with fiat- and gold-backed private digital currencies with applications of cryptography but stumbled over the chicken-egg problem and ran into government interference. Bitcoin, introduced by Satoshi Nakamoto in 2009, was the first non-state, math-backed digital currency to survive its infancy.

PART 2

BITCOIN, THE FIRST CRYPTOCURRENCY

4

BITCOIN HISTORY

HAVING EXPLORED THE NATURE AND CHARACTERISTICS of any monetary system, we'll now focus on the system that interests us most: bitcoin.

Although bitcoin was initially used by only a handful of people, by early 2021, a value equivalent to more than $1 billion was being transacted on the bitcoin network.[37] There are many compelling reasons to use bitcoin. As mentioned in Chapter 1, fiat currencies are based on faith in a national government and its central bank, but backed by nothing. Unlike commodity money, the supply of fiat money is unlimited, as central banks can generate more without constraint. Like gold, bitcoin by design is limited in supply, as well as being faster than wire transfers, mostly anonymous, and extremely secure. The

---

37 "Estimated Transaction Value (USD)," Network Activity, Blockchain.com, accessed December 12, 2022, https://www.blockchain.com/explorer/charts/estimated-transaction-volume-usd.

mystery and genius of its founder barely register as a reason to participate in bitcoin, but they're fascinating and instructive nonetheless.

1. SATOSHI NAKAMOTO

While many people have claimed to be Satoshi, very little is actually known about him.[38] The Satoshi Nakamoto name and identity first appeared on a cryptography mailing list in 2008 and collaborated with several people, none of whom met him in person. Four years and a cryptocurrency revolution later, Satoshi transferred all his software development accounts and other information to software developer Gavin Andresen shortly before vanishing in 2012.

1.i. His Identity

Satoshi included very little biographical or personal information in his posts to the mailing list, and language analysis experts have been able to provide little more. He wrote in English, appears to have been a native speaker, and used an inconsistent mix of British and American spellings and expressions. We can deduce slightly more about his interests.

The mailing list to which Satoshi posted in 2008 was known for its discussion of cypherpunk ideas. As previously mentioned,

---

38   While acknowledging that Satoshi Nakamoto could be female or a group of several people, we use the third-person masculine singular "he" because solo male is the identity Satoshi chose to present. We also follow the community's standard practice of referring to him as "Satoshi" rather than by his second or full name.

cypherpunks favor strong, technology-based privacy as a path to social and political change. The postings on the mailing list covered a range of topics, including mathematics, cryptography, computer science, and political and philosophical considerations.

Satoshi said on the cypherpunk mailing list:[39]

> The root problem with conventional currency is all the trust that's required to make it work. The central bank must be trusted not to debase the currency, but the history of fiat currencies is full of breaches of that trust.

It was on that mailing list and in that context that Satoshi first mentioned he was working on an e-cash system that would accomplish those goals.

Beyond his choice of discussion forum and the legacy of his work, perhaps the most definite hint we have of his motivation (and possibly his nationality) comes from a curious inclusion of text posted in the very first block of the bitcoin blockchain. Satoshi quoted a newspaper headline referencing the then-current financial crisis and the need for another bank bailout, which had run the day of bitcoin's creation in the British newspaper *The Times*.

Satoshi's ownership of the first bitcoins is recorded in the blockchain. One transaction he made was to Hal Finney, a computer scientist and cryptographic activist, and one of Satoshi's first collaborators on bitcoin, and research indicates

---

39 Satoshi Nakamoto, "P2P Foundation: Bitcoin Open Source Implementation of P2P Currency," Satoshi Nakamoto Institute, February 11, 2009, https://satoshi. nakamotoinstitute.org/posts/p2pfoundation/1/.

that Satoshi made very few transactions.[40] Because many are intensely curious about who Satoshi was and where he's been, people have set up bots to monitor those coins.

Figure 4.1: The headline referenced in bitcoin's first block (Source: The Times of London, January 3, 2009, pg 1.)

---

40   Satoshi sent 50 BTC to Hal Finney in this transaction from Jan 12 (UTC time   zone):   https://www.blockchain.com/btc/tx/f4184fc596403b9d638783c-f57adfe4c75c605f6356fbc91338530e9831e9e16.   Gareth   Jenkinson,   "The Value of a Legacy: Hunting Down Satoshi's Bitcoin," CoinTelegraph Magazine, September 1, 2021, https://cointelegraph.com/magazine/2021/09/01/value-of-legacy-hunting-down-satoshi-bitcoin.

1.ii. His Genius

In the years since it was first released, Satoshi's bitcoin code has been examined and analyzed by multiple experts who mostly agree that he wasn't a master programmer. His genius isn't in his code, but in his white paper—in his ability to solve previously insoluble problems using existing pieces of cryptography (called primitives) and combine them in new ways. He came up with a radically original solution to the problem of creating decentralized, secure, digital money.

> **Cryptographic primitives** are well-established, low-level cryptographic algorithms that are frequently used to build cryptographic protocols for computer security systems.[41]

Satoshi saw what was available in other digital money experiments and was clearly aware of even relatively obscure developments in the field. He didn't invent any new cryptographic functions, but took the hashing algorithm from Hashcash, the distributed ledger of B-money, and the cryptographic security that Digicash used. This widespread use and repurposing is significant because, for people involved in cryptography, newer isn't better. Newly invented components haven't been tested enough to be trustworthy. Bitcoin was stronger from its outset for having been made of cryptographic primitives or functions people had already attacked for decades without success.

---

41 Wikipedia, s.v. "Cryptographic Primitive," last modified November 23, 2022, 02:54, https://en.wikipedia.org/wiki/Cryptographic_primitive.

In Chapter 1.2.iii, we introduced the double-spend problem as one that came with the shift from commodity to representative money. In our simplified example, Bob had a hundred dollars in his checking account but wrote one-hundred-dollar checks to two different merchants. His bank honored only the check from the merchant who deposited Bob's check first. Far from ideal, this solution depends on the centrality of Bob's bank. In a decentralized system, it wouldn't work at all.

> **Double-spending** describes a potential flaw in a payment system that allows a person to spend their funds (fraudulently) twice. For example, a person that has USD 100 in their bank account, but writes two checks for over USD 100 would be attempting to double-spend their funds.

In the absence of a single arbiter like a bank, decisions within a decentralized system need to be reached by consensus. Anyone who has tried to reach a collective decision about something as simple as lunch understands this isn't easy to do. The problem of achieving consensus within a decentralized system wasn't new to bitcoin, or even to digital currency. In fact, it was a well-known issue within the computer science community. We'll reserve explaining Satoshi's solution for Chapter 8.3, but no discussion of Satoshi's genius would be complete without mentioning that he was the first to find one.

1.iii. His Agenda

Satoshi laid out a set of well-defined design goals for the new digital currency in his white paper and discussed many of them

on the cryptography mailing list. He wanted to create digital money that functioned as both a currency and a payment
system, and that was decentralized, peer-to-peer, anonymous,
open, scarce, irreversible, and minimally programmed.

Decentralized

Recognizing that every centralized system is, ultimately, based
on trust, Satoshi believed in the importance of decentralization. The risks of centralization are as obvious and simple as
the old cliché: don't put all your eggs in one basket. With one
egg in each of twelve baskets, the loss of any single basket is
recoverable. The risk is distributed, and not much trust needs
to be placed in any one basket-carrier.

Any financial system that relies on a central authority (e.g.,
the company that operated E-Gold) collapses if that single
point of control goes bankrupt, gets shut down, or runs away
with the money. Even if the central authority is controlled by
the state (e.g., central bank), there can be problems such as
debasement of the currency, as we have seen in the previous
chapter. To conduct financial transactions in an environment
of low or zero trust, where individual participants rely only on
themselves and are solely responsible for the security of their
accounts, the system can have no single point of control on
which it depends.

Distributed control wasn't a new idea. The internet itself is
decentralized. An outgrowth of a Defense Advanced Research
Projects Agency (DARPA) project called ARPANET (Advanced
Research Projects Agency Network), the internet's infrastructure was developed in the 1950s under the shadow of possible

nuclear attack. A robust national communications system, the defense department recognized, would need to avoid what computer scientists call a **Single Point of Failure (SPOF)**, a vulnerability in which the failure of one portion of the system renders the entire thing inoperable.

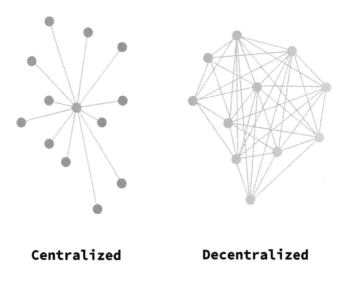

Centralized   **Decentralized**

Figure 4.2: Relationships between participants in centralized and decentralized network configurations

Imagine what happens to the network if the central dot in the left image fails. Every other dot (called a **node**) is completely disconnected, every connection breaks, and no one can communicate with anyone. In the right-hand, decentralized configuration, there is no node whose loss would cripple the network.

If the defense department's entire communication network had its hub in Washington, DC, a nuclear strike against the nation's capital would make any nationally coordinated response impossible. Having had small foretastes of this disruption when transatlantic communications cables had been inadvertently severed by ships, DARPA designed the proto-internet to be decentralized from its inception. Happily (if ironically), the same decentralization built into the early internet by the government to protect it from foreign attack makes it equally impervious to government take-down.

Having seen ventures as diverse as the Liberty Dollar and Napster collapse when their controlling organizations ran afoul of the US government, Satoshi also saw decentralization as a shield against such state interference. He was explicit about this, saying in one 2008 mailing list post: "Governments are good at cutting off the heads of centrally controlled networks like Napster."

Napster

In the early 2000s, as music started being released in digital form, people began to use the internet to share and trade song files. Napster established itself as a clearinghouse service that offered a central location to facilitate such sharing, which the music industry viewed as theft. People who bought a digital copy of a song owned the right to listen to it, but not to make copies to share, trade, or sell. Because most such copies were stored on and distributed through Napster servers rather than by and between individuals, the company became the target of multiple lawsuits and government action and was shut down.

Re: Bitcoin P2P e-cash paper

Satoshi Nakamoto   Fri, 07 Nov 2008 09:30:36 -0800
>[Lengthy exposition of vulnerability of a systm to use-of-force
>monopolies ellided.]
>
>You will not find a solution to political problems in cryptography.

Yes, but we can win a major battle in the arms race and gain a new territory of freedom for several years.

Governments are good at cutting off the heads of a centrally controlled networks like Napster, but pure P2P networks like Gnutella and Tor seem to be holding their own.

Satoshi

The Cryptography Mailing List
Unsubscribe by sending "unsubscribe cryptography" to

Figure 4.3: Satoshi's commentary on decentralized systems (Source: Satoshi Nakamoto, "Re: Bitcoin P2P E-Cash Paper," November 7, 2008, https://www.bitcoin.com/satoshi-archive/emails/cryptography/4/.)

Peer-to-Peer

Peer-to-peer structures within a decentralized system allow individual components of that system to communicate directly with one another, providing resilience against failures of or abuse by a "middle man" intermediary.

Peer-to-peer: Most frequently used to describe the interaction of computers within a network, any peer-to-peer system allows for direct interactions between participants without the need for a hub or centralized mediation.

Creating anything close to peer-to-peer banking required an entirely new and separate financial system, since building such a structure within the world financial framework would be functionally impossible. Individuals are simply unable to carry out unmediated transactions more complicated than a simple sale or purchase between themselves.

As an example, if Alice wanted to provide banking services for herself and her extended family, she would need to apply for a license. She would also have to put a technical infrastructure in place to access the SWIFT (Society for Worldwide Interbank Financial Telecommunication) network through which the world's financial institutions communicate. Alice would have to spend millions, and she couldn't do it herself. In other words, if she (or any of us) wants banking services, we can't rely on ourselves. We must use a bank. If the banks refuse to serve her or process transactions she makes, she's functionally cut off from the transfer of fiat money.

Society for Worldwide Interbank Financial Telecommuni-cation (SWIFT): an international system using standardized message syntax to communicate money transfers between banks.

In all these examples, transactions can be monitored, censored, or prohibited because they must flow through a central point that is sensitive to government pressure. In a peer-to-peer network, that oversight becomes impossible because the inter-mediary is missing. Participants conduct transactions directly. Alice needs no one else's involvement or permission to send bitcoins to her half-cousin in Russia or to make a contribution to WikiLeaks.

Software Updates and the Bitcoin Protocol

Bitcoin is "backward-compatible" in that all bitcoin data is recognized by the latest bitcoin software. Satoshi designed bitcoin in such a way that new versions of its software are deliberately backward-compatible. Changes to it can augment but may not invalidate older iterations. Without a corporate headquarters to officially release and impose updates, people can continue to use years-old versions of the bitcoin software, creating a remarkable diversity of software versions operating within the bitcoin community. Bitcoin developers continue to work on the software, but users cannot be forced to use updated versions. Users of software written by centralized organizations can be compelled to update software in order to continue to use it.

> **Protocol:** A set of rules accepted by compatible clients (e.g., email can be sent between Gmail, Outlook, etc.).

Most users, however, adopt the latest version to employ new additions to the protocol that are almost universally accepted.

Pseudonymity

As part of the cypherpunk community (which advocates privacy-enhancing technologies), it's not surprising that Satoshi included mechanisms for privacy in his design agenda. Bitcoin, in the parlance of cryptocurrency, is *not* genuinely anonymous but pseudonymous, for reasons we'll discuss in Chapter 5.3.iv. However, it still offers much more protection of personal privacy than conventional payment systems do.

> **Pseudonymity:** the use of pseudonyms rather than names to identify individuals and accounts.

A bitcoin account is a bit like a Swiss-numbered account used to be.[42] If a register of all numbered Swiss bank accounts and of all transactions between those accounts were made public, anyone could see that Swiss Bank account number X holds Y dollars and has carried out transactions of A and B dollar amounts with account numbers C and D. There would,

---

42 Swiss bank accounts ceased to be anonymous in 2018.

however, be no way to know from that register who owns account X. In this example, however, the bank would have information connecting the person to an account number and could, conceivably, be compelled to release it. In bitcoin, the blockchain is the equivalent of that publicly released register, but there is no equivalent to the bank. No one holds a record of whose name is associated with which account numbers.

People keep their bitcoins in bitcoin wallets (to be explained in more detail in Chapter 6.2), but by design, no information stored on the blockchain links people to these wallets. Individuals can access the bitcoins in their own wallets, but nobody else knows that key to unlock the wallet or who owns the wallet. Nowhere is a person's name tied to their wallet. Still, bitcoin isn't truly anonymous since some information about the status and activities of each account is publicly accessible.[43]

Open Development

Satoshi wanted to develop the bitcoin system as "open source software," meaning that everyone should be able to check how the system works. If Satoshi would have included a secret part in the software that no one can check, this would have limited trust in the system. Developing everything openly has several advantages:

---

43   Monero and Zcash are examples of more anonymous cryptocurrencies, in which only the people involved in a transaction know it's occurred. If the participants so choose, transactions will show very little information about the participants and amounts in the transaction.

1. Other people can check the code, and, if there are
   mistakes in the codebase (often referred to as "bugs"),
   the chances are higher that someone will eventually
   find them.[44]

2. Being able to check how the system works helps to
   build trust in the system, which is very important
   when creating a new currency and payment system.

3. Often people studying the code find improvements or
   help implement features, meaning that an open-source
   approach recruits additional (often highly skilled)
   developers who contribute to the code.

Scarce

Recognizing the same reality that the music industry had
tripped over—that digital properties can be inexpensively
replicated with complete fidelity—Satoshi built scarcity
directly into bitcoin. Not only can individual bitcoins not be
copied (because the public ledger records the creation and
tracks the movements of each one), but Satoshi also designed
the system to stop producing new ones. He set the maximum
number of bitcoins at 21 million, with the last one expected to
be created in 2140. In Chapter 8.4.i, we'll discuss how that limit
is enforced, but for now, it's enough to say that Satoshi, aware

---

44 In software development, this observation is called Linus' Law and is often
summarized as "given enough eyeballs, all bugs are shallow." Eric S. Raymond
described his observations of open source development in his famous essay "The
Cathedral and the Bazaar" [Eric S. Raymond, "The Cathedral and the Bazaar," in *The
Cathedral & the Bazaar: Musings on Linux and Open Source by an Accidental Revolutionary* (Sebastopol, CA: O'Reilly, 2001), 19–64].

that scarcity is a critical trait in a currency, explicitly designed a mechanism to cap the production of bitcoin at a predetermined maximum.

Irreversible

It was important to Satoshi that bitcoin operate more like cash than most other digital payment systems. Cash is irreversible. For example, if Alice gives Bob twenty dollars for a box of dog food, only to get home and find the box empty, there's not much she can do. However, if she paid for her kibble by credit card or PayPal, she could dispute the charge and possibly get her money back.

Reversibility offers consumers a certain degree of protection. Satoshi could easily have built structures into bitcoin that allowed transactions to be reversed indefinitely or within a limited number of completed blocks. He chose not to, in part, to make bitcoin more cash-like, but also because the ability to dispute transactions requires adjudication. Without an intermediary, transfers for legitimate purchases could be fraudulently reversed as easily as fraudulent transactions could be legitimately undone. It might be possible to create a system of arbitration within a decentralized network, but not without incurring expenses that would necessarily be passed along to users as fees.

Satoshi wanted bitcoin to be a viable method for making small, casual transactions and believed the cost of such mediation would limit the minimum transaction size. Perhaps even more significantly for him, he believed that reversibility required trust and reduced privacy. Any system that assumed the risk of refunding purchases would be motivated to vet the vendors to whom it sent payments and to investigate both the identity and legitimacy of people requesting refunds.

Minimized Feature Set

Satoshi wrote bitcoin's code to resist the inclusion of any features beyond those necessary to perform the tasks he designed it to do. This parsimony reduces the risk of programming errors. On the software level, bitcoin transactions are carried out by specific chunks of programming code called scripts. Satoshi chose simple scripts to conduct a tightly limited number of operations. This leanness in bitcoin's programming contributes to the stability of the network while still allowing participants to do more complex things than simple A to B transactions.

2. BITCOIN'S RECEPTION

Bitcoin: A Peer-to-Peer Electronic Cash System

Satoshi Nakamoto
satoshin@gmx.com
www.bitcoin.org

Abstract. A purely peer-to-peer version of electronic cash would allow online payments to be sent directly from one party to another without going through a financial institution. Digital signatures provide part of the solution, but the main benefits are lost if a trusted third party is still required to prevent double-spending. We propose a solution to the double-spending problem using a peer-to-peer network. The network timestamps transactions by hashing them into an ongoing chain of hash-based proof-of-work, forming a record that cannot be changed without redoing the proof-of-work. The longest chain not only serves as proof of the sequence of events witnessed, but proof that it came from the largest pool of CPU power. As long as a majority of CPU power is controlled by nodes that are not cooperating to attack the network, they'll generate the longest chain and outpace attackers. The network itself requires minimal structure. Messages are broadcast on a best effort basis, and nodes can leave and rejoin the network at will, accepting the longest proof-of-work chain as proof of what happened while they were gone.

1. Introduction

Commerce on the Internet has come to rely almost exclusively on financial institutions serving as trusted third parties to process electronic payments. While the system works well enough for most transactions, it still suffers from the inherent weaknesses of the trust based model. Completely non-reversible transactions are not really possible, since financial institutions cannot avoid mediating disputes. The cost of mediation increases transaction costs, limiting the minimum practical transaction size and cutting off the possibility for small casual transactions, and there is a broader cost in the loss of ability to make non-reversible payments for non-reversible services. With the possibility of reversal, the need for trust spreads. Merchants must be wary of their customers, hassling them for more information than they would otherwise need. A certain percentage of fraud is accepted as unavoidable. These costs and payment uncertainties can be avoided in person by using physical currency, but no mechanism exists to make payments over a communications channel without a trusted party.

What is needed is an electronic payment system based on cryptographic proof instead of trust, allowing any two willing parties to transact directly with each other without the need for a trusted third party. Transactions that are computationally impractical to reverse would protect sellers from fraud, and routine escrow mechanisms could easily be implemented to protect buyers. In this paper, we propose a solution to the double-spending problem using a peer-to-peer distributed timestamp server to generate computational proof of the chronological order of transactions. The system is secure as long as honest nodes collectively control more CPU power than any

Figure 4.4: The first page of Satoshi's white paper (Source: Satoshi Nakamoto, "Bitcoin: A Peer-to-Peer Electronic Cash System," Bitcoin.org, October 31, 2008, https://bitcoin.org/bitcoin.pdf.)

2.i. The White Paper

When Satoshi posted his white paper, "Bitcoin: A Peer-to-Peer Electronic Cash System," to the cryptography mailing list in November 2008, it was not an overnight sensation. In fact, most list participants' reaction was a lukewarm "Yeah, that's kind of cool," and Satoshi had some trouble convincing anyone to try out the first version.

It's hard to imagine. In a single, slender document, Satoshi had proposed a revolutionary idea that was almost fully formed at its creation. And almost no one noticed. He found some early encouragement from Hal Finney, but the two men struggled to engage other participants, and bitcoin nearly died in its first year from lack of interest.

After the white paper that laid out all his ideas, Satoshi wrote the computer program that implemented them. Then he started minting these new coins, a process that is also known as "mining." The first bitcoins came into existence with the creation of the first block (called the genesis block). Satoshi sent several of them to Hal Finney in the world's first bitcoin transaction on January 12, 2009.

Genesis block: the name of the first block of a blockchain (e.g., bitcoin).

The bitcoin genesis block (see Figure 0.1) contains the newspaper headline of *The Times* (cf. Figure 4.1) "Chancellor on brink of second bailout for banks."

For more than a year, bitcoin was little more than an interesting game played among an extremely small group of cryptography enthusiasts. They literally gave it away. Gavin Andresen (to whom Satoshi would eventually turn over bitcoin's core systems) set up a website, Bitcoin Faucet, which gave anyone who entered their email address 0.01 bitcoins for free.

It wasn't until another party on the forum accepted 10,000 bitcoins (also known as BTC) to deliver two large pizzas, which he bought with fiat currency, that bitcoin had any real value.[45] It crossed that defining moment and became a medium of exchange for two people. Until that transition, bitcoin had struggled with the chicken/egg quandary that ultimately defeated DigiCash: why should bitcoin (or any other currency) ever have value? All currency is an abstraction, and with the possible exception of items that are themselves useful (like cigarettes), money has no intrinsic value. Even precious metals, without collective agreement on their desirability, have no physical utility—they aren't edible and provide neither shelter nor warmth.

---

45   This fateful purchase was made on May 22, 2010, now commemorated within the community as Pizza Day.

Figure 4.5: The two large pizzas ordered for 10,000 BTC (Source: Bitcoin Wiki, "Laszlo Hanyecz," last modified May 7, 2017, https://en.bitcoin.it/wiki/Laszlo_Hanyecz.)

Digital currencies are even further removed from the direct satisfaction of survival needs. Digital money is just code in computers, and bitcoin, because its code is freely available, illustrates the psychological component of money even more starkly. Anyone could copy its software and, with minimal changes, create their own version. Alice could create Alice-Coins, which would have every property a bitcoin does, but she probably couldn't convince Bob to accept 10,000 Alice-Coins for two pizzas. Bitcoin, however, is worth approximately $50,000 a piece, as of December 2021, on the strength of the faith placed in its utility, its math, and its "brand."

2.ii. Early Valuations

Once even a small group of people realized that they could buy real-world goods with bitcoin, they had a benchmark value—at that point, approximately 0.0025 US cents. Until that moment, people had only theoretical constructs based on how much a bitcoin costs to produce. After the initial pizza purchase, interest in bitcoin was also fueled by its interesting and novel features, including its built-in scarcity.[46] People began buying it not to use, but to hold onto in the (subsequently justified) hope it would appreciate, using it as a "store of value."

TIMELINE	
3 January 2009	Bitcoin created
12 January 2009	First bitcoin transaction
22 May 2010	Pizza day
17 July 2010	First bitcoin exchange opens

In 2010, exchanges such as Bitcoin Market and Mt. Gox began to open. It became easier to purchase and sell bitcoins, and price discovery became more transparent. On July 11, a popular computer-news website called Slashdot published an article on a newly released version of bitcoin that increased interest within a broader community. With wider adoption and interest, the price of bitcoin increased quickly, as the following chart illustrates (note the logarithmic scale on the y-axis). However, the increase was not smooth, but exhibited some very fast surges and dips in the first few years.

---

46   We will see in Chapter 8.4.i why there will only ever be 21 million bitcoins.

Bitcoin Price

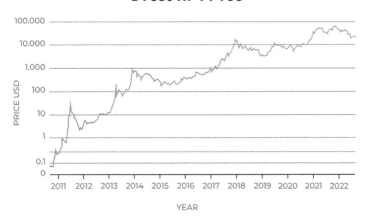

Figure 4.6: Bitcoin price over time (note the logarithmic scale of the USD price)

2.iii. Volatility

In 2012, a person buying a million dollars' worth of bitcoins would have a significant effect on its price. Today, that same million wouldn't make much of a blip. That million would buy fewer bitcoins (because the price has gone up) and represent a much smaller percentage of the overall market (because there are more bitcoins available). In short, the volatility of the bitcoin market depends, in part, on its size and age.

Today, we still see large fluctuations in bitcoin prices, but they no longer rise and fall so precipitously or range so widely. In the first ten years of its life, from 2010 to the present, a single bitcoin has gone from having no financial value, to being worth .0025 cents, to being worth orders of magnitude higher.

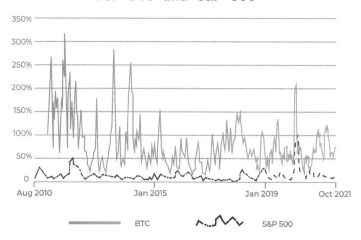

Figure 4.7: Annualized historical volatility of bitcoin (BTC) and the S&P 500

In the early days, bitcoin's price didn't correlate strongly with traditional assets as reflected in the various stock markets. Bitcoin's massive price movements at the ends of 2013 and 2017 weren't simultaneous with big price explosions in American stocks or other world markets.

Although bitcoin's volatility has decreased significantly, the speed and degree of price change still keep it from being an extremely effective medium of exchange. As of April 2021, people buy and trade it primarily as a store of value, much the way they do gold.[47]

---

47   Like gold, bitcoin is scarce. Unlike gold, the precise amount of as-yet unmined bitcoin is known.

2.iv. Early Participants

Bitcoin's early participants were, in attitude, closer to explorers motivated by curiosity and idealism than to the hard-driving tech entrepreneurs of Silicon Valley startups. In many of the relatively obscure early-interest-group mailing lists, there was an almost playful attitude toward the experiments they carried out within their small communities. The stakes were low, and much of bitcoin's early history only makes sense through the lens of people more interested in experimentation than the exigencies of wealth creation.

Similarly, in those early years, the first bitcoin exchanges required very little identification beyond an email address—not because they were setting up black market operations, but because they were playing a "let's see what happens if" game. It was in that spirit that Laszlo Hanyecz managed to convince someone to trade him pizza for bitcoins, and the same level of low-stakes experimentation is evident in Gavin Andresen's Bitcoin Faucet.[48] Today, bitcoin is worth so much money that it's become a serious business.

We started using bitcoin between 2011 and 2013, and worked on various software projects to support the growing ecosystem. Also we recognized that mining new coins was very profitable, and thus, we ordered several graphic processing units (GPUs) and started our first mining operation.[49]

---

48   The Bitcoin Faucet issued free bitcoins to interested parties on request.

49   In this specific case, we mined litecoin with GPUs.

Bitcoin mining is the name for the process of minting new bitcoin by solving very difficult mathematical problems with the help of computers. Both in gold and bitcoin mining, physical energy is used to extract a valuable resource—hence the use of the term *mining*.

It did well enough that when we learned another friend had access to warehouse space in Bosnia-Herzegovina, we bought significantly more GPUs, shipped them over, and set up our first farm in 2013.

This took longer than we initially expected, and we made the beginners' mistake of buying different kinds of the hardware we required, like GPUs and motherboards, rather than standardizing by using as few hardware variants as possible. It was very chilly, so the extra heat generated by our equipment gave us an added incentive to work quickly. The end result was a hot, loud, enormous room stuffed with blinking LEDs. We were up and running. We were mining bitcoin!

2.v. Mainstream Attention

By early 2013, millions of dollars' worth of bitcoins were being bought and sold each day, and it was no longer an experimental pursuit among a small subset of an obscure interest group. In October of that same year, the FBI raid of Silk Road, an online black marketplace, brought bitcoin even more into the public eye.[50]

---

50 Silk Road used bitcoin as a means of payment and is covered in more depth in Chapter 5.4.vii.

Bitcoin and Governments

Most of bitcoin's early adopters were aware of (and several directly involved in) earlier digital experiments like Napster, E-Gold, and the Liberty Dollar, which had been shut down by the US government. Understandably, in the early days of bitcoin, there was a great deal of uncertainty about its legal status and concern over how regulators might react.

Government authorities issued warnings, cautioning that cryptocurrencies were risky and less stable than the national fiat currency.[51] Many articles were written warning of and predicting the imminent or eventual collapse of bitcoin.[52]

Some people heeded those warnings and stayed away, but as bitcoin gained mainstream attention, many people, weighing their options, recognized that it ultimately was a question of trust. Some, even as they lost a bit of their money every year to inflation, kept all their trust in the central banks that issued unbacked fiat money, promising to control it in a way that would benefit end-users. Others bought into the new mathematics-backed currency.

Despite its volatility and newness, enough people decided for bitcoin that, in the spring of 2013, its total value (or more precisely its "market capitalization") had reached $1 billion.

---

51 For example, the central banks of New Zealand, China, and others warned about bitcoin in 2013 [Rebecca Howard, "New Zealand Central Bank Joins Others in Warning on Bitcoins," *Wall Street Journal*, December 11, 2013, https://www.wsj.com/articles/BL-REB-21982; Robin Sidel, Chao Deng, and William Horobin, "Central Banks Warn of Bitcoin Risks," *Wall Street Journal*, December 5, 2013, https://www.wsj.com/articles/china-central-bank-warns-of-bitcoin-risks-1386234633].

52 "Bitcoin Obituaries: Bitcoin Has Died 467 Times," 99Bitcoins, accessed December 12, 2022, https://99bitcoins.com/bitcoin-obituaries/.

Market capitalization (often referred to as "**market cap**") is the product of a company's outstanding shares times the current market price per share. For example, if AliceCo Inc. has one million outstanding shares and the shares are currently trading at US$100, then AliceCo Inc. has a market cap of US$100 million.

While the concept is primarily used to value companies in the stock market, the same concept is often used to value (and compare) cryptocurrencies. For example, as of April 2021, there were approximately 18.7 million bitcoins in circulation, each of them trading at about US$60,000, resulting in a market cap of about US$1.1 trillion.

In November of that year, several bitcoin experts were called to testify before the US Congress.[53] The event was a successful debut for bitcoin in that institution, with officials and witnesses highlighting the innovative aspects and novel use cases of bitcoin, without ignoring its potential criminal uses.

Other national governments have taken a dimmer view of cryptocurrency. While, at the time of writing, it is legal to own and trade bitcoin in the US and EU states, it is illegal in some other countries. Different countries have different approaches to regulating bitcoin, so that users have to inform themselves, depending on the jurisdiction, which rules apply in their situation.

---

53 Timothy B. Lee, "This Senate Hearing Is a Bitcoin Lovefest," *Washington Post*, November 18, 2013, https://www.washingtonpost.com/news/the-switch/wp/2013/11/18/this-senate-hearing-is-a-bitcoin-lovefest/.

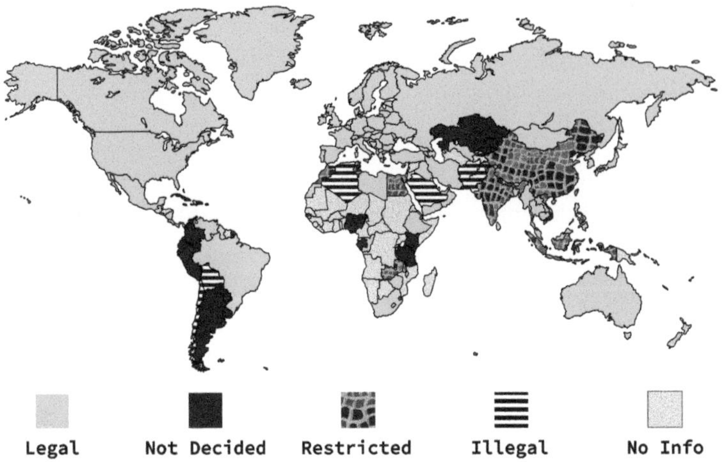
Legal
Not Decided
Restricted
Illegal
No Info

Figure 4.8: The above map shows the legal status of bitcoin worldwide as of 2022 (Sources: Evangelina Chapkanovska, "Bitcoin Regulation: Where Is Bitcoin Legal?," SpendMeNot, April 4, 2022, https://spendmenot.com/blog/bitcoin-regulation/; "Global Bitcoin Political Support and Public Opinion," Coin Dance, last modified March 22, 2021, https://coin.dance/poli).

Financial Institutions

Bitcoin's early reception from commercial banks and other financial institutions was a studied indifference. Few in the financial sector understood its underpinnings, and bitcoin's relatively small size meant that banks saw little reason, or were simply unable, to participate. Besides, there is inherent risk in any new and experimental technology.

Traditionally, banks are in general conservative, highly regulated, and risk-averse. Bitcoin has a number of (from a bank's perspective) unusual and unfamiliar features, and integrating these in the banking operating procedures and IT takes a lot of time and effort. For example:

- A bank is obliged to verify the identity and some other personal information of its customers; bitcoin has no such barriers to entry.

- A bank is able to reverse a transaction, for example in the case of theft or fraud, but in bitcoin there is no way to do this.

- Bank accounts are held by known natural or legal persons, whereas bitcoin addresses are pseudonymous.

- Banks are regulated by national financial regulators, but bitcoin, as open source and decentralized software, is steered by participants in the community.

- Storing large amounts of bitcoin for clients needs a very secure and specialized protection system.

Given these major differences to the traditional banking world and the relatively small market size of bitcoin, banks did not see that integrating bitcoin was worth the effort.

On the other hand, several small financial technology ("fintech") startups began to integrate bitcoin and other cryptocurrencies, and in order to be able to interact with the conventional finance system, adopted some of the procedures in traditional finance (such as KYC/AML). In addition, some smaller financial institutions, trying to gain an advantage by engaging with a more innovative form of finance, tried to adapt and win cryptocurrency firms as clients or offer cryptocurrency services to customers.

> **Know Your Customer (KYC):** a process that obliges most banks and insurance companies to check who their customers are and where their funds originate from.
>
> **Anti-Money Laundering (AML):** a set of controls and procedures primarily adapted by financial institutions to prevent, detect, and report money-laundering activities.

2.vi. Cryptocurrency Ecosystem

As with any major innovation (like smartphones and cars), competitors started to pop up everywhere. Initially other projects copied the bitcoin code base or only made minor modifications to it; however, a few years later cryptocurrencies were released that were completely written from scratch.

- In April 2011, namecoin, a software that was directly derived from the bitcoin source code, was published. Namecoin was the second cryptocurrency in existence, and its main differentiator was its intent: create a decentralized registry for domain names.

- Litecoin was published in October 2011. It was an early spinoff of bitcoin, and except for a few modifications (primarily faster processing time and a different way to mine it), it was identical to bitcoin.

- Ethereum was released in July 2015 (its founders include Vitalik Buterin, Gavin Wood, and Charles Hoskinson). While the underlying mechanism for reaching consensus in a decentralized system was conceptually similar to bitcoin, it was much broader in the sense that bitcoin only allows the transfer of one type of token (called bitcoin), while Ethereum allowed every participant to create their own new token and to define their behavior (e.g., tokens that represent stocks).

Since the release of bitcoin in January 2009, more than ten thousand cryptocurrencies have been released, most of which have failed. However, bitcoin was the spark that formed a whole new ecosystem of cryptocurrencies and decentralized systems that quickly became worth hundreds of billions of US dollars.

CHAPTER SUMMARY

Although his identity remains uncertain and obscure, Satoshi Nakamoto's genius is self-evident and incontestable. He proposed and built the world's first cryptocurrency, which today, a mere ten years later, has a market capitalization of over $1 trillion. Perhaps even more impressively, he engineered an entirely new form of money.

Money, an abstraction whose utility makes it ubiquitous throughout human civilization and across cultures, evolved over thousands of years before Satoshi re-conceptualized it. He did this deliberately, in service to ideals grounded in a belief that money, a foundational economic good, could be better. To him, and many others after him (including the four of us), the requirements of "better" include an integrated currency and payment system that is decentralized to protect against single points of failure. Better money decouples economic activity from faith in systems that have historically been misused at times, and it bases its value in mathematics rather than government fiat. It also satisfies the functions of money while maximizing its positive traits. To see how bitcoin accomplishes all this, let's examine its structure more closely.

5

BITCOIN STRUCTURE

Satoshi created bitcoin to redress many of the short-comings he saw in the evolution of digital money from fiat currencies. Designed from first principles, bitcoin has always had significant advantages over traditional money systems. To better understand bitcoin's strengths and advantages, as well as its issues, we should explore its structure and examine how it performs as both a currency and a payment system.

Somewhat confusingly, as previously mentioned, "bitcoin" is used to refer both to its single unit of currency in the way we talk about the US dollar (e.g., Alice has five bitcoins) and to its payment system in the way we talk about bank transfer or a service like PayPal (e.g., Alice used PayPal to send Bob five dollars. Alice used bitcoin to pay him.)

In Chapter 2, we defined a currency as a unit of value and a payment system as a method of transferring that value between people. Yet, bitcoin as both a currency and a payment system was foundational to Satoshi's design, which gives it a coherence lacking in fiat currency—especially in its digital manifestations, where the various payment systems have scrambled to carry their physical forms of security into the digital space.

1. BITCOIN CURRENCY

In Chapter 2.2, we listed six traits of money: scarcity, divisibility, durability, portability, fungibility, and security. In Chapter 2.3, we assessed cowry shells, rai stones, Roman denarii, and cigarette money against those traits. Here, we'll apply the same criteria to bitcoin.

1.i. Scarcity and Security

As mentioned in the previous chapter, Satoshi recognized scarcity as an essential currency trait and explicitly designed a mechanism to keep people from making multiple copies of a single bitcoin, meaning that a single coin could not be duplicated and spent twice. He also set 21 million as the maximum number of bitcoins ever to be produced. Unlike fiat money—the supply of which can be increased almost at will—the amount of bitcoin, like that of gold, is finite.

We don't know exactly what percentage of the earth's precious metals have already been mined or how many cowry shells are left undiscovered, but there will never be more than 21 million bitcoins. Of that 21 million, approximately 18.9 million have been mined as of December 2021. Thus, if Alice buys one bitcoin, she can be sure it will always be one of only 21 million in the world. With 7.9 billion people alive today and many more to be born, Alice will always have, in her one bitcoin, something incredibly scarce.

Since bitcoin isn't mined from the ground, its scarcity doesn't come from dwindling natural reserves in increasingly inaccessible places, but from a mathematical constraint. Satoshi set a limit on how many new bitcoins could be created within each (approximately) four-year period between its inception and the year 2140.[54] To ensure a logarithmically decreasing number, the number of new bitcoins in each four-year period is half of the number mined in the previous four-year period. To simplify this idea, it's useful to think in dollars and months rather than in bitcoins and years, and to imagine a less abstract situation where the available supply of newly mined bitcoins is halved.

Let's say Bob is trying to wean his son off his parental income. At present, young Charlie gets eighty dollars a month. On Satoshi's reduction model, after four months, Charlie's allowance would drop by half, from eighty to forty dollars a month. Four months later, it would be halved again to twenty. At the beginning of the second year, Charlie would be getting only ten bucks a month for the first four months, then five in the next four and finally $2.50 a month by the end of the second year. By that time, we hope he's making enough on his own that what he gets from Bob no longer makes much of a difference.

Of course, the cap Satoshi created on the total number of bitcoins would do nothing to guarantee scarcity if bitcoin were

---

54 This four-year period is not actually measured by time elapsed but by the number of blocks created. For reasons we'll discuss in Chapter 8.2.v, the amount of time it takes to make a new block stays relatively constant at about ten minutes.

easy to counterfeit. But bitcoin, like the enormous rai stone disks, is immune to theft because ownership is established as a matter of public record. The islanders maintained an account in their collective memory of each stone's provenance and history. Bitcoin records the same information (and more) in a public ledger. It's impossible to counterfeit bitcoin not only because this would be incredibly difficult technically, but also because any attempt would be immediately evident to all bitcoin participants and the network, which would reject the fakes automatically.

1.ii. Divisibility

Increased divisibility is one of the significant advantages that allowed paper money—and by extension fiat money—to replace commodity money. Bills of different denominations allow for one hundred dollars to be divided into as few as two bills or as many as a hundred. Coins allow for further fractions of the dollar, which is still monolithic in comparison to bitcoin.

Bitcoin is divisible to eight decimals (10^{-8} or 0.00000001), with one bitcoin consisting of one hundred million Satoshis. (This smallest possible unit of bitcoin was named after bitcoin's founder.) This high degree of granularity means that bitcoin, even in the event of a large fiat currency devaluation, could still be used in day-to-day transactions. This granularity also provides excellent protection against currency devaluation. Even if bitcoin becomes the world's leading currency, it's hard to imagine it becoming so valuable that merely moving a decimal wouldn't easily accommodate its growth. For example, when a single bitcoin is worth $10,000, the one ten-thousandth of a bitcoin (0.0001) is worth one dollar. If its value soared to $100,000, the dollar equivalent would simply add a zero. No previous currency has been remotely as divisible.

Satoshi: the smallest division (one one-hundred-millionth) of a bitcoin.

1.iii. Durability

Bitcoin isn't flammable, and it doesn't wear out or shatter if dropped. Further, because the network is distributed, the ledger—which establishes that a bitcoin exists and is valid—exists simultaneously on thousands of computers across the world. The only element of bitcoin potentially subject to physical damage is a (completely optional) physical method of storing one's **private key**.

Private Key: an alphanumeric fifty-two-character string, similar to a password, needed to transfer bitcoin.

In order to use bitcoins, you need a private key. The currency's real durability rests on how safely you store these. Different methods exist, including storing different parts of the private key in different locations. We'll discuss the importance of these private keys and offer recommendations about their safe storage in the next chapter and explain how they work in Chapter 6.3.

1.iv. Portability

In the same way that the digital nature of bitcoin makes it profoundly more divisible than any previous representative or fiat currency, there's also no contest on the trait of portability. No matter the number of bitcoins in a transaction, all that's required to carry it out is a string of letters and numbers (the private key) small enough to write on the back of a fortune cookie fortune. (But please don't!)

1.v. Fungibility

Bitcoin resembles gold in its fungibility. In the same way that one newly smelted ounce of pure gold is worth the same as any other, every new bitcoin is of equal value.

People have created tools to analyze where individual bitcoins originated and how they've been used. For example, if bitcoins were recently transferred from an illegal online marketplace (such as "Silk Road"), these bitcoins might be labeled as "tainted."[55] If an institution can identify particular bitcoins as originating from illegal sources, as found by blockchain-analysis software, they may refuse to accept them.

Reputable exchanges (more on this in Chapter 6.4.i) analyze the origin and recent usage of the bitcoins they receive, and thus the risk of receiving "tainted" coins from such an exchange is very low.

---

55 Note that there is no generally accepted standard that defines the meaning of a "tainted" coin.

Although the fungibility of bitcoin is not perfect, in day-to-day usage it is very high, and it is unusual for issues to occur for this reason.

1.vi. Comparison of Traits

Now that we have established the traits of bitcoin, we want to check how they compare against those of other currencies, most importantly fiat and gold (cf. Chapter 2.3.vi).

	Gold	Fiat	Bitcoin
Durable	**++**	**++**	**+**
Portable	**+**	**+**	**++**
Fungible	**+**	**+**	**+**
Verifiable (Resistance to counterfeiting)	**0**	**-**	**++**
Divisible	**0**	**+**	**+/++**
Scarcity	**+**	**-**	**++**

Figure 5.1: Comparison of traits of bitcoin, fiat currency, and gold

From the table it becomes clear that bitcoin's traits as a form of money are excellent, and especially better than those of fiat or gold. Maybe that's not too surprising as its creator had the benefit of studying thousands of years of monetary history and all its failures, and could design bitcoin for the purpose of being money's best possible form.

Bitcoin's underlying traits make it an excellent form of money.

2. THE BITCOIN PAYMENT SYSTEM

Having previously covered the more philosophical reasons why a decentralized, peer-to-peer framework was important to Satoshi, we'll now look more deeply at the bitcoin payment system's structure and implementation and compare it to previous payment systems.

2.i. Decentralized and Peer-to-Peer

All fiat currencies are under the control of the power by whose fiat they were created. For example, the US dollar is under the control of the Federal Reserve, which sets the rules for money creation and determines what percentage of its deposits a commercial bank must hold in reserve. While the existence of multiple credit card companies and digital payment systems like Venmo and PayPal create some consumer choice, they still must abide by the Federal Reserve rules to be able to deal in US dollars. Further, each of these individual payment systems is, itself, centralized. The government could shut any of them down as easily as it did Napster. Peer-to-peer transactions of fiat currency, of course, are still possible.[56] Bob can pay Alice $100 directly in cash, but if he wants to pay her $100,000, he's going to have trouble doing so without government oversight.

All fiat currencies are under the control of the power whose fiat or decree created them.

In bitcoin, the only limit on how much Bob can send directly to Alice without the involvement of a third party is the number of bitcoins he owns. While we'll discuss the security of the bitcoin payment system later, it's worth noting here that being decentralized contributes to the resilience of the system. Nothing depends on a single point of potential failure. The entire system exists on thousands of computers, all of which fulfill the same function.

2.ii. Transactable

Similarly, all large transactions and most international ones are easier to conduct with bitcoin than with fiat currencies. While most banks instantly credit deposits under a certain threshold, larger ones frequently require a waiting period of hours or days. Wire transfer requests can only be placed during regular banking hours, and international transactions are subject to scrutiny by and the regulations of every country involved. Further, even sending (or receiving) relatively

---

56 As long as physical cash still exists and is not entirely replaced by digital transactions.

low dollar amounts within one's own country requires opening a bank account, which, in turn, requires providing a lot of personal information.

The dollar is much more widely accepted than bitcoin. From observing the bitcoin transaction count, it can be seen that the number of use cases of bitcoin is growing. Many people unfamiliar with cryptocurrency are intimidated, expecting that, since the theory behind bitcoin can be complicated, the system itself is challenging to use. While it's true that the mechanisms that underpin bitcoin are relatively sophisticated, the operations involved in using it are no more complex than sending and receiving email.

2.iii. Secure

In Chapter 2.4 we discussed the importance of the security of payment systems, for protection against fraud and theft. When the payment system involves physical items like shells or coins, it is important to be able to protect them, for example from being stolen.

Decoupling value from objects (as rai stones did) or providing for some reversibility (as credit cards do) can improve a system's security. However, for the most part, until bitcoin, payment systems relied on stringent controls and limited access for security. This "security through obscurity" mindset traveled with money as it became digital in the form of closely guarded algorithms, firewalls, and encryption. Unfortunately, any security mechanism that relies on other parties not knowing how it works is not only vulnerable to hacks, it almost invites them. Bitcoin, in contrast, is open protocol and open source and much more secure as a result.

2.iv. Open Protocol and Open Source

While there are multiple email clients, there isn't an Email Inc. that regulates or licenses them. Instead, there's an agreed-upon set of rules that allow a person with a Gmail address to send and receive emails with someone using Outlook. Rule sets such as these are called protocols, and they may be open (public) as in our email example or proprietary and secret, as Skype's are. Anyone who wanted to could write their own email client that, provided it followed the established protocols, would be as able as any other to send and receive email.

> **Protocol:** a set of rules that determines how two or more parties (in most cases computers) within a communications system transmit information. A rule set can be either public or private. In the case that it is public, it is referred to as a **public protocol**.

While protocols are rule sets that allow parties in a communication system to interact with one another, source code determines how the individual programs behave. Like protocols, source code may be open (publicly available) or closed (kept secret). Outlook uses open protocols, but its source code is not open. If it were, anyone who wanted could create an email client that was identical to Outlook.

In bitcoin, the source code and protocols—which govern how computers in the bitcoin network communicate with each other, what information they exchange, how transactions are configured, and what constitutes a block—are open. With so many people watching the bitcoin network and invested in its success, if anything in its code updates ever goes wrong, they'll likely find and fix it before any malicious actors could exploit it.

> **Open Source:** publicly available source code that governs the operation of computer programs or software.

As mentioned in the previous chapter, this kind of openness mattered to Satoshi on principle. Part of his agenda was to create a financial system that didn't require people to put their trust either in governments or other users. Bitcoin is open source so that participants can convince themselves individually that there's no way the system can be hacked. Now, after withstanding more than ten years of both well-intentioned and malicious attempts to break it, bitcoin's security is about as proven as can be.

2.v. Public Ledger

Bitcoins, like rai stones, are almost impossible to steal. The enormous size of rai stones required a payment system that decoupled ownership from physical possession. Instead, ownership was entrusted to a public ledger kept in the collective memory of the islanders, which recorded the story of each stone's creation and all transactions made with it. Bitcoin weighs nothing at all and leaves little to memory, yet it also records the creation and transactions made with each bitcoin in a public ledger called a blockchain. We'll discuss what this is and how it operates in Chapter 8. For the moment, let's just say that the blockchain contributes to the security of the bitcoin payment system in that it's decentralized because it is housed on every computer in the bitcoin network. A hacker would have to convince most owners of copies of the blockchain to change their versions of it to his advantage—an all-but-impossible task.

3. PROPERTIES OF BITCOIN

As both a payment system and a currency, bitcoin has significant advantages over every prior currency we've studied.

3.i. Uptime

Uptime is important to digital payment systems. Most frequently expressed as a percentage, it contrasts uptime (those minutes or hours during which the system is online and operational, expressed as a percentage of total time) with downtime (in which the system is down, inaccessible, or unusable). Tech companies like Google and Facebook maintain a very high, close to 100 percent uptime. Banks, in contrast, regularly take their systems down for maintenance or make certain operations (like wire transfers) unavailable during particular hours. Bankers' hours themselves (nine to five, Monday through Friday) would mean an uptime of only 26.8 percent. Bitcoin, partially because it is decentralized, has extraordinarily good uptime. It is usable almost all the time.

Even if multiple computers crash or an entire country's internet goes out, bitcoin continues to operate on other machines. Since it was launched, bitcoin has enjoyed a >99.99 percent uptime.[57]

3.ii. Transaction Fees

To prevent fraud and maintain security, a payment system must establish the legitimacy of the transactions it enables. In other electronic payment systems such as PayPal, bank transfers, and credit cards, the company (PayPal, the bank, or the credit card company) acts as an intermediary that essentially vouches for legitimacy (the sender is the rightful owner of the account) and sufficiency (there are adequate funds in the account to cover the request). These companies assess fees to cover the cost and risk of their verification processes.

Since bitcoin is decentralized, the task of validating the legitimacy and authenticity of transactions falls to other members of the network. In addition, all transactions need to be processed in order to be confirmed. This is also referred to as "mining." Those who do this work are compensated. At present, this compensation comes in two forms: the creation of new bitcoins (which we discuss in more detail in Chapter 6.5.iii), and the transaction fees paid by the originator of the transaction.

While the practice of assessing transaction fees isn't new to bitcoin, the calculation of how they're assessed is. In

---

57 In March 2013, bitcoin experienced a chain split incident, during which it was not safely usable for six hours.

conventional financial transactions, the amount paid in fees for high-value international transactions is often based on a percentage of the amount of money being exchanged. Therefore, the larger the transaction, the higher the fee. This is not the case in bitcoin. It costs the same to send $10 or $10 billion worth of bitcoin, with the price of fees established dynamically to reflect the real-time demand for transactions and paid directly to the people doing the work of validating the transactions and entering them into the bitcoin register.

Miners can select which transactions to validate based on the fee being offered. This will be discussed in detail in Part 3. While at any given moment, there is a typical market price for fees, it fluctuates in response to the overall volume of transactions. The higher the demand for transaction validation, the higher the average fee.

A miner is:

1. a person or entity that runs specialized computer hardware to validate transactions on the bitcoin blockchain.

2. the specialized hardware itself.

Mining is the process of validating a batch of transactions (called a "block"), which allows the miner to mint (or "mine") new bitcoins.

A person who wants to carry out a bitcoin transaction is essentially competing for a miner's services against everyone else who wants to do the same. This person can effectively raise their bid by offering a higher fee, increasing the likelihood that their transaction will be selected by a miner and validated more quickly. People can time their transactions to take advantage of lulls in the market or raise their fee post hoc if they subsequently decide the work is going too slowly.

Bitcoin transaction fees are transparent and set by the user, independent of transaction value.

3.iii. Stability

History often repeats itself, and, over the thousands of years since the Roman denarius, the money supply often becomes corrupted or debased. The Roman government steadily reduced its currency's silver content, and countries including Germany and Venezuela have seen their currencies become worthless at different points in their histories. While the precipitating causes may include war, civil unrest, and governmental policy, the primary cause of a currency's collapse is always a breakdown of the faith placed in its stability and continued ability to perform its functions, particularly as a store of value. Proponents of cryptocurrency, recognizing that all currencies and economies require people to place their trust in something, opt for faith in mathematics over governments, hence the bitcoin motto *vires in numeris* (strength in numbers)!

Because the precise number of bitcoins that remain to be mined is known, algorithmically defined, and fixed in the software, its future supply is much more predictable than that of gold or any other precious metal. There is no way to tell how much gold is left in the earth. There is even less certainty about the future fiat money supply, since more can be created by both central and commercial banks by fiat and through the practice of fractional reserve banking.

Although it doesn't entirely shelter bitcoin from the risk of government interference—a drawback we'll discuss in Section 4.viii below—decentralization does protect bitcoin from government seizure.

3.iv. Pseudonymity

In Section 1.iii of Chapter 4, we introduced the term "pseud-onymous" to describe bitcoin relative to Satoshi's design agenda. We suggest that bitcoin's pseudonymity is somewhere between "transparent" and "anonymous."

Figure 5.2: Comparison of degree of privacy of bitcoin and cash

However, this anonymity is not absolute, as the transaction record is public and associated with pseudonyms. This balanc-ing act alone is enough to qualify bitcoin's pseudonymity as an advantage, but to understand the positive aspects of pseud-onymity, we need to study it more carefully.

Authors use pseudonyms or pen names to screen their iden-tity. Many early female novelists took male pen names so that they would more easily find a publisher for their work. Many contemporary authors use multiple names to differentiate their work by genre.

In bitcoin, each account is identified by a pseudonym, in the form of a very large number assigned to the account holder. Every bitcoin transaction is recorded in the public ledger, with the sending and receiving accounts identified only by these single large identifying numbers. However, the use of pseud-onyms does not guarantee anonymity, which makes bitcoin a poor cryptocurrency choice for criminals.

Bitcoin does not use the real names of participants (like a bank does if you open an account) and is therefore not fully transparent. Instead, bitcoin accounts (of which everyone can create an arbitrary number) are referred to by (random) alphanumeric characters.

A **bitcoin address** or **bitcoin account** is an alphanu-meric identifier for an account that holds bitcoin (very similar to a bank account number). For example: "bc1qsjdlsn5thw0edj3des7wcqcj6ujj2xy5uz3gac"

An image would be helpful to understand exactly what is happening. Let's imagine Alice has ten bitcoins that she stores in two different accounts, each of which has a unique, pseud-onymous address (see Figure 5.3).

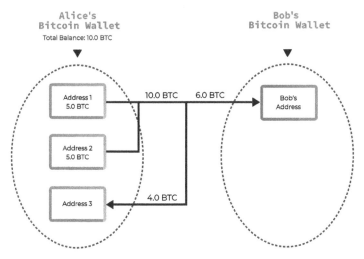

Figure 5.3: Alice's bitcoin wallet transfers 6.0 BTC to Bob's wallet.

Assuming she's divided her bitcoins evenly, if she wants to send Bob six bitcoins, she could create a transaction that takes bitcoins from both accounts. For Eve, watching the transaction from the outside, Alice's two accounts are now linked in such a way that it is indisputable that one person owns them both. Eve can't know that person is Alice, and Eve also cannot know whether Bob received six bitcoins or the four remaining. Due to the mechanics of bitcoin transactions, all of the coins must be sent, and then the remaining coins are returned as change to the sender, but if Alice is a criminal and Eve part of the police force, she can start piecing together what Alice has been doing—who's sending bitcoins to her and whom she's sending it to. If Eve can then connect Alice to even one account, she could potentially unravel the ownership and activities of several other of her accounts.

Bitcoin's pseudonymity, while providing more privacy than traditional banking systems, isn't identity-obscuring enough to make it as attractive to criminals as some more truly anonymous cryptocurrencies are. Bitcoin therefore has a mix of transparency and privacy, with a public transaction ledger but pseudonymous account holders.

4. ISSUES WITH BITCOIN

Of course, nothing is perfect, and a thorough examination of bitcoin would be incomplete without a careful examination of its relative downsides. While we personally believe the following issues are either acceptable risks or drawbacks that can be successfully mitigated, it's important that readers understand bitcoin's issues. Here, we've broken potential problems into risks (issues that might pose a threat to the system) and drawbacks (characteristics of bitcoin that are less than ideal), with a final third subsection devoted to reputational risk—the usage of bitcoin in darknet markets.

The risks associated with bitcoin fall roughly into two categories: human and technical. Bitcoin is at risk of both human error and abuse, and it is also vulnerable to several technical threats. Risks associated with bitcoin potentially pose a threat to the network. Drawbacks are more subjective. Some are the downsides of otherwise positive features; others are considered benefits by some.

For newcomers, bitcoin's price volatility can be psychologically difficult to adapt to. Since that volatility is much higher, in fiat currency terms, than that of traditional investments such as stocks, property, and precious metals, the large price movements that occur can cause a degree of anxiety. Over the long term, such nervousness tends to diminish as experience with holding bitcoin develops.

4.i. Possibility of Errors

The more complicated code is, the more likely it is to contain errors, which programmers call "bugs." Not only does the value of bitcoin make it an attractive target for hackers, the simple fact of its security and success is a provocation. To a hacker, bitcoin is an uncrackable bank vault full of diamonds. Code is, after all, written by people, and people make mistakes—although bugs can also be inserted deliberately into code by ill-intentioned programmers. Either way, bugs can have serious implications. Mistakes in programming can be exploited by viruses (malicious code written by other programmers), which can be used to gain unauthorized access to systems, to crash applications, or to steal personal and financial information.

Considering that bitcoin is both complex and the first of its kind, it is quite possible—even probable—that its code is somewhat less than flawless. In fact, several issues have already arisen since its introduction in 2009. In August 2010, an overflow bug was discovered that could have potentially begun creating new bitcoins two hundred years from now, well after the time new bitcoin creation is to be capped at a total of 21 million coins. In March 2013, an update to bitcoin code caused the bitcoin register to split unintentionally into mutually exclusive forks. Bitcoin network participants quickly resolved this problem by reverting back to the older version.

Possible programming errors can also be counted as one of bitcoin's drawbacks. In much the same way that a cataclysmic meteorite strike is a drawback to life on earth, it's possible, if unlikely, that a bug might cause some bitcoin nodes to behave incorrectly. Bitcoin is a technology whose limits still need to be explored, and there may be bugs or shortcomings that have not yet been discovered. However, it's done remarkably well for over a decade.

4.ii. Technical Risks

In the future, certain portions of bitcoin's core structure could be made obsolete by technical or mathematical advances. As we have written before, bitcoin uses certain tested building blocks called cryptographic primitives. While these have been well tested, these cryptographic primitives sometimes get weaker or fail, due to mathematical or computational advances. For example, quantum computers may in the future make bitcoin more vulnerable to cryptographic attacks. Bitcoin security depends on a particular type of cryptography called elliptic-curve cryptography, which mathematical advances could conceivably render inoperable. Likewise, the emerging field of quantum computing has the potential to crack bitcoin's cryptography and disrupt the consensus algorithm on which it depends. Bitcoin however has in principle the ability to update its cryptographic primitives in order to maintain its security.

Finally, as we mentioned in Section 1.ii of the last chapter, Satoshi Nakamoto relied heavily on time-tested building blocks, which could fail at some point. If they do—if these so-called computer primitives are ever successfully attacked—not only bitcoin will be affected. For some such building blocks, like elliptic-curve cryptography, the consequences would be far-reaching, disrupting things as commonplace as the HTTPS protocol on which website and email security rely.

Bitcoin was followed by clone cryptocurrencies using the same or similar principles, of which Namecoin was the first. Because bitcoin's source code is open, many other organizations and individuals have developed new cryptocurrencies on its foundation. They've added new features and experimented with a wide variety of alterations that the bitcoin community did not wish (or could not afford) to try. To date, this has been more to bitcoin's benefit than its detriment, as bitcoin has been able to take on new elements that have been tested and proven to be both stable and useful, while avoiding the risks associated with undertaking such experimentation.

Risk of Fracturing through Community Dispute

We explained in Chapter 4.1.iii that bitcoin is a protocol that has to be followed by all participants. However, if some participants would start using a modified version of the bitcoin protocol (e.g., allowing 100 million bitcoins instead of 21 million bitcoins), this would result in two branches: one that follows the original protocol, and one that follows the new protocol.

A (hard) fork is a split of the bitcoin network resulting from participants following different protocols.

The biggest example of a hard fork is so-called "bitcoin cash." However, in terms of number of developers, market capitalization, and number of transactions, this is only a small fraction of the size of bitcoin.

The possibility exists that unresolved disputes in the bitcoin community could cause parts of the community to separate and continue with their own forks, thus dividing the network and causing resources to be taken away from bitcoin.

Conservative Development Approach

Bitcoin's programming and development philosophy is quite cautious and conservative. Additionally, because both bitcoin and its developers are decentralized, there is no hierarchical chief to make definitive decisions about when or whether to introduce new features, or what solution to implement when problems arise. Most of the people involved have firmly held opinions, and consensus around such topics can be challenging to find. In fact, many new cryptocurrencies have their origin in schisms amongst bitcoin developers.

High Energy Usage

For reasons we'll go into in Chapter 8.2.iv, the bitcoin network burns terawatts of electricity with millions of devices purpose-built for bitcoin mining in operation world-wide. Other projects are working on solutions that consume less energy, but maintain the same level of security and decentralization. However, it is unlikely that bitcoin would deviate from its current, well-tested method. As we've said, bitcoin is, by temperament and organizational structure, very conservative and slow to change. A move away from "proof of work" in bitcoin's consensus mechanism would be a more radical alteration than any the network has undertaken thus far.

The consumption of electricity fundamentally links bitcoin to the physical world, a link not present in other solutions. Even if there were a better system, it would still be a new and untested one competing with the over-ten-year track record of the present implementation. Finally, many of the people who'd need to agree to such a shift are heavily invested in existing machines despite their electricity cost. It's hard to imagine them voting against their own interests.

We'll discuss the economics of bitcoin mining in Chapter 8.4, but electricity is, by far, the highest operating cost miners incur. Any reduction in what they pay for energy would increase their bottom line.

4.iii. Abuse

Beyond mistakes in the code like the two we've just mentioned, it's also possible to misuse the system to its detriment. Whenever an attacker reaches a majority of the mining hardware, this could result in a so-called 51 percent attack.

A 51 percent attack is a potential attack on the bitcoin network that requires a bit more than 50 percent of the bitcoin mining hardware, and hence is called a 51 percent attack. Acquiring enough mining hardware to perform a 51 percent attack would be extremely expensive.

This will be further discussed in Chapter 8.3.iv. An attacker that controls 51 percent of the mining hardware would have the possibility to disturb the network, e.g., by intentionally excluding transactions (censorship), by modifying the order of transactions, or by reversing transactions.[58] However, the attacker would not be able to steal bitcoin from user wallets.

4.iv. Illegal Content

In much the same way that paper checks have a memo field in which people can write a short message, bitcoin allows users to include a small amount of additional information in their transactions. While this can have useful applications, for example for time stamping, in the past, some malicious network participants have used this option to include illegal content like links to child pornography or controversial WikiLeaks documents that then become a part of the blockchain. Because the blockchain is permanent and distributed, this information then technically lives on the computers of every network participant, putting them in possession of something illegal. If there are any pictures stored on the blockchain, they

---

58 Also, the possibility of a miner attack with less than 51 percent of total mining power was published in 2013.

are stored in patches and are not easily accessible but would require special decoding methods to extract them. In practice, we are not aware of any practical enforcement activities by the authorities on this basis.[59]

4.v. Lack of Appeal

In Chapter 4.1.iii, we discussed bitcoin's irreversibility and decentralized structure. While these traits were important design goals for Satoshi, there is a related downside. Irreversibility combined with decentralization means there is no way to undo a mistake, and the cost of even a small error can be very high.

As an example, say Bob gets access to any of Alice's private keys and empties the associated accounts (information on how to avoid this is in Chapter 6.3). Because bitcoin is decentralized, there is no third party or central authority to whom Alice can appeal, and because bitcoin is irreversible, there is no way for her to get the stolen coins back. Likewise, if, fearful of theft, Bob secures his private keys so thoroughly that he can't find them himself, there's no way for him to recover them, and all the coins he had in his account are permanently lost. In fact, the value of "lost" bitcoin is estimated to be in the billions. A man in Wales famously threw out a hard drive with 7,500 BTC on it.

Bitcoin is very failure-intolerant in this area. If someone misplaces the PIN for his debit card, he can reset it. If someone

---

59 "A Quantitative Analysis of the Impact of Arbitrary Blockchain Content on Bitcoin," Blockchain Content Research, ComSys, RWTH Aachen University, accessed December 12, 2022, https://blockchain.comsys.rwth-aachen.de/.

steals it, the bank will often refund the fraudulent charges. There is no similar fallback or failsafe for bitcoin users.

As we saw in Chapter 3.3, despite being the first cryptocurrency, bitcoin had predecessors that it eclipsed, and the same thing could happen to it in the future. There is a risk that a new form of currency—one that is more technically advanced—could overtake bitcoin in the same way Facebook overtook MySpace.

4.vi. Fractional Reserve Banking

While a much less egregious form of abuse, it's important to note that bitcoin is not intrinsically immune to the practice of (and consequent devaluation caused by) fractional reserve banking. In the future, if banks or other institutions accept cryptocurrency deposits, they could operate the same practices we discussed in Chapter 1.2.iii, holding only a percentage of the bitcoin deposited with them and lending the rest to borrowers. For bitcoin, it is possible to make transparent the reserves being held, thus making it possible to prove whether a fractional reserve scheme is being run.

4.vii. Reputational Issues

A reputational issue for bitcoin is its use for illegal activity. The unregulated nature of bitcoin may have attracted criminals, since transactions do not go through the conventional financial system. Other positive features of bitcoin, such as its portability, appeal not only to the law-abiding but to criminals. Nonetheless, the US dollar still continues to be used for most drug transactions. From 2011 to 2013, Silk Road was an online marketplace specializing in illegal goods and services. At that time, as one of very few cryptocurrencies, and by far the biggest, bitcoin became the coin of the realm on Silk Road. That's the only connection between them.

Silk Road was hosted on the darknet (sometimes called the Tor or Onion network), which deliberately makes it very hard to trace a website back to the location of its hosting server. Since this is the typical path taken by law enforcement to remove sites and prosecute the people involved in illegal online activity, the darknet was almost custom-tailored for criminals.

Recognizing a business opportunity in this, Ross Ulbricht, under the pseudonym "Dread Pirate Roberts," set up Silk Road as a marketplace where prospective buyers and sellers of illegal goods could find each other, make deals, and rate one another's reliability. Almost everything was available for sale, but the vast majority of purchases were of marijuana.

The site operated for a little under three years before the FBI caught up with Ulbricht and shut down Silk Road. While he argued that he only was involved for the first few months of the website's existence, and that he handed over the operation to others unknown, the courts disagreed and sentenced him to life in prison without the possibility of parole. The FBI raid and Ulbricht's subsequent trial received an enormous amount of media attention, and bitcoin got some portion of that as the primary currency used on Silk Road.

Interestingly, however, with the possible exception of public opinion, none of this had a lasting negative impact on bitcoin. The price dropped on the day of the raid, but four days later, it was back to within a few dollars of what it had been. Of even greater significance, the loss of this entire segment of the crypto economy caused the number of bitcoin users to dip by only 5 percent.

4.viii. Possibility of Government Interference

In the beginning, there were often no laws covering bitcoin, but now many jurisdictions have enacted regulatory regimes of varying natures for cryptocurrencies. It's difficult to predict how well or even whether it will be accepted by central banks and states around the world. We are optimistic because, while most countries have been somewhat less than enthusiastic, few have declared it to be illegal. Many are now creating regulatory frameworks intended to hold bitcoin to rules like those they apply to fiat money.

CHAPTER SUMMARY

Both open protocol and open source, bitcoin is a currency that is scarce, highly divisible, durable, portable, and mostly fungible. It is also a decentralized, easy to use, and secure payment system that outperforms its predecessors on all these metrics. An engineered rather than evolved system, bitcoin adds almost perfect uptime; equitable, market-driven transaction fees; political and economic security; and pseudonymity to its list of advantages.

It is, nevertheless, a system engineered by humans and consequently imperfect. There are risks and drawbacks to bitcoin, and it has been used for illegal activity. We believe these issues are small compared with the tremendous potential of a mathematics-based, peer-to-peer digital currency that has grown exponentially with remarkably few serious setbacks and has operated successfully for over ten years.

With a solid grounding in what money is, how it works, and why we think bitcoin is its best and most advanced manifestation, we hope readers are now ready to jump down the rabbit hole and explore how bitcoin works in greater depth.

PART 3

HOW BITCOIN WORKS

6

BITCOIN FUNDAMENTALS

To fully comprehend bitcoin's potential and limitations, it is important to understand some of the underlying fundamental concepts, which this chapter will introduce.

1. TERMINOLOGY

1.i. On Bitcoin Addresses and Private Keys

Let's say Alice wants to receive mail. She can sign up for a post office box. Anyone to whom she gives her post office box number can send mail to her. To retrieve her mail, however, Alice must unlock her mailbox with the correct key.

The equivalent for the post office box number in the bitcoin world is a **bitcoin address**. A bitcoin address is a unique alphanumeric sequence of 26–35 characters.[60] For example:

- 1BvBMSEYstWetqTFn5Au4m4GFg7xJaNVN2

- 3KE8HQxTSP7aH9sksA36YnrZFHbU4rCkHw

- bc1qar0srrr7xfkvy5l643lydnw9re59gtzzwf5mdq

are all valid addresses that can be used to receive bitcoin. In practice you almost always copy and paste these addresses, or transfer them using QR codes, without having to type every character of the full address.

A few notes on bitcoin addresses:

- All bitcoin addresses start with a "1," "3," or "bc1." These refer to different types of addresses that were introduced over time. The technical details are not relevant for everyday use.

- A bitcoin address can be imagined as a bank account number, where your bitcoins (instead of your US dollars or euros) are stored.[61]

---

60 The characters used within a bitcoin address are fewer than the maximum possible. This collection of characters is called base58. Usually, you would expect the whole alphanumeric alphabet (a-z, A-Z, 0-9), which is in total 62 characters, to be used; however, as the characters 0, O, "l" (small "L"), and "I" (capital "i") in some fonts look very similar, these were removed to avoid potential mistakes.

61 This view is a bit simplified but helps in understanding the basics. In reality, bitcoin internally does not have "accounts" but only tracks transaction outputs and whether these are "spent" or "unspent" (cf. Chapter 6.2.iii).

- An error detection is built into the address, so in (the rare) case where you have to type an address, it is extremely unlikely that a typo will result in a valid address. This helps to prevent sending bitcoins to the wrong address.

- A user can generate an arbitrary number of bitcoin addresses.[62]

- Some people refer to a "bitcoin address" as a "public key." While in practice this will seldom cause difficulties, this is not accurate, and the distinction will be explained in Chapter 7.3.ii.

A post office box number is represented by a bitcoin address. However, if Alice wants to access her post office box, she needs a key for that. The equivalent in bitcoin is a **private key**, which is a randomly generated 256 bit number that can be represented as a string of case-sensitive letters and numbers, e.g.,[63]

5KEDgoVfAn7esdjrsC3pymSNk6YJJA4K7ybBl4
A2fHZkAvHHGCW[64]

---

62 Note that this does not require centralized coordination (which would be a no-go, as bitcoin is designed as a decentralized system). You might wonder how it can be avoided that Alice and Bob by chance generate the same address. The reason is that the address space is so large that Alice and Bob would (almost certainly) not generate the same address even if they both generated addresses nonstop on super-computers for millions of years.

63 A bit is the most basic unit of information in computing, most often described as either "0" or "1." The term "bit" is a combination of the words "binary" and "digit." The name was invented by John W. Tukey.

64 Private keys start with a "5" (which is purely a convention to make them easily recognizable).

Alice's post office box key only allows her to access exactly one post box. In a similar way, a private key can only be used to access one bitcoin address. For example, the above private key is directly connected to the bitcoin address 12nkwt47FKmz-1KL7BJLed3XrbDS2CyKnV5. That address can be generated from the private key. In other words, a private key allows a user to access the corresponding bitcoin address, in order to spend the bitcoin stored at that address.

As the name suggests, the private key *must* be kept private. This is absolutely critical to protect your bitcoins. Later we will discuss a number of good solutions that are available for users to help them secure their private keys and thus their bitcoins.

In the case of Alice's post office box, if someone else has her key, he can also access her post office box. If Alice loses the key, she also cannot access the box and loses what she had stored in it, or what anyone has sent to her there. Similarly, anyone who has the bitcoin private key can access the bitcoin address and spend the bitcoins stored in it. Losing the bitcoin private key means that the bitcoins stored at the corresponding address are irretrievable.

1.ii. The Bitcoin Ledger

A person or business can use a ledger to record account balances and transactions with business counterparties. Historically these were paper records (see Figure 6.1), but nowadays ledgers are maintained digitally using specialized software.

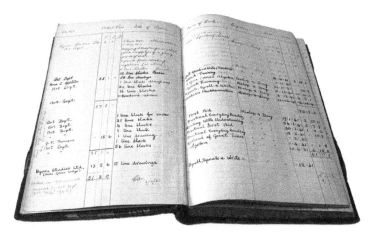

Figure 6.1: A traditional ledger (Source: Wikimedia Commons s.v., "Ledger Detailing External Work Commissioned at Holmes McDougall," last modified September 17, 2020, https://commons.wikimedia.org/wiki/File:Ledger_detailing_external_work_commissioned_at_Holmes_McDougall_(4268190563).jpg.)

Every computer that participates in the bitcoin network (known as a "bitcoin node") stores a copy of the list of bitcoin addresses, and the number of bitcoins stored at each address. This list is known as the "bitcoin ledger." An example of a bitcoin ledger is shown in Figure 6.2, with the names rather than the addresses being shown for readability. This is a rather simplified explanation in order to introduce the concept of the bitcoin ledger, and we will explain the details further in a later section. The second graphic illustrates that an identical copy of this ledger is held and maintained by thousands of machines worldwide, thus decentralizing the system extremely effectively and contributing to its robustness.

Ledger	
Dave	12.5 BTC
Alice	323 BTC
Bob	6.2 BTC
Carol	10 BTC
...	...

Figure 6.2: A simplified depiction of the bitcoin ledger (Source: CuriousInvestor, "How Bitcoin Works in 5 Minutes (Technical)," April 14, 2014, YouTube video, 5:25, https://www.youtube.com/watch?v=l9jOJk30eQs.)

The bitcoin ledger is public. Anyone can connect to a bitcoin node and download the whole bitcoin ledger without restriction. As the bitcoin ledger contains the whole history of all addresses and their past and current balances, all bitcoin transactions that have ever been carried out are available for anyone to see.

The bitcoin ledger is a bit like the communally held record of rai stone ownership. Distributed across the nodes of the bitcoin network, the ledger records the creation and every transaction of all bitcoins in existence. Like the giant stone disks, bitcoins never actually move anywhere. Their ownership is simply assigned and reassigned. When new bitcoins are mined, their creation are noted in the bitcoin ledger, as is the address to which it was assigned.

The bitcoin ledger is:

- a public ledger that keeps records of all account balances and transactions,

- distributed to thousands of computers (also referred to as "nodes"),

- only showing account addresses, not the names of their owners ("pseudonymity").

Ultimately the bitcoin ledger is where (your) bitcoins are stored. Full copies of the ledger are held on thousands of computers all around the world.

1.iii. Bitcoin Transactions

Let's look at what steps occur when Alice sends one bitcoin to Bob. Again, we will simplify the process slightly at this stage and provide more details later.

1. Using her wallet software, Alice generates a transaction (using her private key), which is then sent to the bitcoin network.

2. All bitcoin nodes, which make up the bitcoin network, do various checks on Alice's transaction, for example: whether Alice has one bitcoin to spend, and that Alice is the bitcoin's owner, and that Bob's address is valid.

3. Through a process called "mining" (again to be explained later), the bitcoin network reaches consensus whether to include Alice's transaction on the bitcoin ledger.

4. On all bitcoin nodes, the bitcoin ledger is updated, and Alice's bitcoin now belongs to Bob.

Figure 6.3: Alice transfers 1.0 BTC to Bob.

This is the simplest form of transaction possible on the bitcoin network. However, more complicated transactions are also possible: for example, a transaction where the sender sends bitcoin to more than one recipient address (e.g., Alice sends 1.0 bitcoin to Bob, and 0.3 bitcoins to Carol).

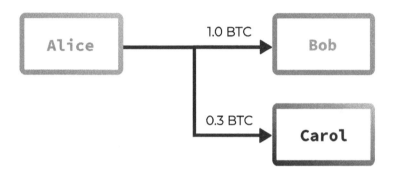

Figure 6.4: Alice transfers 1.0 BTC to Bob and 0.3 BTC to Carol in one combined transaction.

It is also possible for Alice to combine several of her accounts in order to make a transaction. (As mentioned below in section 2.ii, bitcoin users often have multiple addresses.) In case Alice wants to send one bitcoin to Bob, but none of her addresses have sufficient bitcoins, she can easily combine several addresses.

All of this usually happens automatically in the background of the bitcoin wallet software, without extra effort on Alice's part. From her perspective, she will only see her total wallet balance (the total held by all the bitcoin addresses in her wallet), i.e., 1.3 bitcoins prior to the transaction in Figure 6.5.

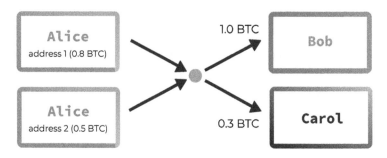

Figure 6.5: Alice combines two of her addresses in one transaction.

Again, it is important to understand that, unlike transactions in conventional financial systems, once the transaction has been carried out, it is *irreversible*. It cannot be revoked. In the conventional financial system, if there had been some mistake with Alice's transaction, she could contact her bank and ask for it to be reversed or canceled. Due to the decentralized nature of bitcoin, there is no equivalent of the bank for Alice to contact, and no possibility for her to reverse the transaction, other than asking Bob to send the bitcoin back.

2. BITCOIN MANAGEMENT

A user needs to be able to perform the basic bitcoin functions easily, with a tool that automatically manages more complicated tasks, such as having multiple addresses. For this, a bitcoin wallet is used, which makes the interaction with bitcoin user-friendly and helps avoid mistakes, which in the worst case could lead to bitcoins being lost. This can be used in a way similar to an online bank account, with the ability to send, receive, and store bitcoins.

2.i. Bitcoin Wallet

A **bitcoin wallet** is used to administer bitcoin private keys and the associated bitcoin addresses for the user. In its simplest form, you can imagine it as a set of bitcoin private keys (and the corresponding bitcoin addresses).

Figure 6.6: Alice's bitcoin wallet has four addresses.

A **bitcoin wallet** is a program or service that stores and manages a collection of bitcoin addresses that belong to the same user. Most wallets allow a user to send and receive bitcoins.

Most bitcoin wallets also allow users to send and receive bitcoin. Furthermore, some wallets offer advanced functionality, e.g., support for cold storage, selecting a reasonable transaction fee, or cryptographically proving the ownership of funds.

A bitcoin wallet can be installed as PC software or loaded onto a mobile phone or a tablet as an app. In these cases, the bitcoin addresses and private keys are stored on that device, often in an encrypted form. This means that if someone steals the files storing the private keys, they cannot be used by the thief unless they are decrypted. In the online version, a service provider stores bitcoin with its own private keys for its users. In this case, you have to trust a third party to hold your bitcoins safely. You must ensure that the service provider is itself trustworthy and has sufficient security systems in place not to be hacked.

Once a user has installed a bitcoin wallet, the first step the wallet will carry out is to generate bitcoin private keys and addresses. As we will explain later, users generally have more than one address in order to make it more difficult to trace their activity, increasing the user's privacy. A user can then have bitcoin sent to those addresses, and the wallet will then monitor and record these transactions. Once the user is ready to send bitcoins, the wallet can generate that transaction. For security, wallets often have passwords, PINs, and encryption systems to protect users' bitcoin holdings.

Although there are multiple addresses being held by the bitcoin wallet, a user does not need to interact with the individual addresses themselves. They can simply deal with the total account and its balance without having to be concerned how the balance is split among the individual addresses. For example, to send 3.3 bitcoins, a user only needs to set up a 3.3 bitcoin transaction once, and the software will create transactions involving the multiple addresses required, without any further user intervention (cf. Figure 6.7). Furthermore, individual addresses that had but no longer have any bitcoin in them are still actively managed by the software, which will recognize if in future transactions bitcoins are sent to them, and will update the total wallet balance accordingly.

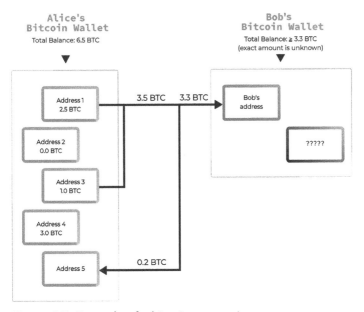

Figure 6.7: Example of a bitcoin transaction

Bob is probably also using a bitcoin wallet. However, Alice knows very little or almost nothing about it, except that it includes Bob's bitcoin address. Someone observing the transaction (which is public) will learn that an individual has spent bitcoins from "address 1" and "address 3" in a single transaction, and thus can be fairly certain that these belong to the same bitcoin wallet.

However, from the outside, we cannot know whether "address 5" is also part of the same bitcoin wallet. An observer from the outside does not know if 3.3 BTC were sent to Bob, and 0.2 BTC back to Alice's wallet, or vice versa. It could even be that 3.3 BTC were sent to Bob and 0.2 BTC to Carol, or that the 3.3 BTC as well as the 0.2 BTC were both sent back to Alice. Bob of course knows about his address and most likely also about the reason for the transaction, so he can assume (although not be 100 percent sure) that "address 5" is part of Alice's wallet.

The above is an example and reminder that bitcoin transactions are not completely anonymous. Some information (in this case "address 1" and "address 3" belonging to the same wallet) can be deduced. There are companies that perform "blockchain analysis" on this open information to try and understand who owns which wallets and who transacts with whom.

There are services that can help users enhance their privacy. One example of this, which most bitcoin wallets offer, is the use of change addresses.

2.ii. The Change Address

Whenever Alice is doing a transaction, it will be part of bitcoin's transaction history, which is publicly available. This might result in privacy issues, e.g., if Alice were only to use one address for all of her bitcoin transactions. If she keeps reusing her address, her transaction parties could easily identify when Alice is spending bitcoin and how much. They might not be able to see who Alice's counterparty is (although in many cases a bit of analysis might reveal even that), but they certainly would know how many bitcoins Alice possesses.

Instead of reusing the same address again and again, it is best practice to use bitcoin addresses only once. Most bitcoin wallets will create a new so-called **change address** on the fly, and send the remainder of the funds to that address. All this happens under the hood and most users will not even notice it.

Bitcoin best practice: do not reuse bitcoin addresses.

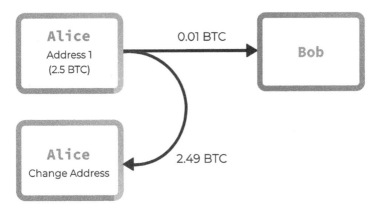

Figure 6.8: When sending 0.01 BTC to Bob, Alice sends the remaining BTC in address 1 to a separate change address.

Besides privacy concerns, there is another reason for not reusing a bitcoin address: the security of a bitcoin address that was already used is slightly weaker, though still reasonably strong for most purposes.[65] However, it has become a best practice for bitcoiners to use addresses only once.

---

65 For an unused bitcoin address, an attacker would have to "reverse" two different hashing functions to determine a public key and then find a private key for that public key. A used bitcoin address has already revealed its public key. However, finding a private key from a public key alone is practically an insurmountable hurdle. For more details, please see Chapter 7.3.ii.

2.iii. Accounts and UTXOs

Previously, for simplicity's sake, we talked about bitcoin addresses as if they behaved much like checking accounts, but the parallel isn't exact. If Tassilo wires two hundred dollars to Helen's checking account number 1234, which already had one hundred dollars in it, when Helen checks her balance, it will show three hundred dollars. If Tassilo sends Helen two bitcoins to her bitcoin address 5678, and she already has one bitcoin that she bought, she won't have three bitcoins at her address on a bitcoin exchange. Instead, the bitcoin software keeps track of the two transaction outputs that she has not spent so far:

1. the 1 bitcoin transaction output from the exchange, and

2. the 2 bitcoins from Tassilo's transaction output

The outputs of the transactions that were not yet spent are also referred to as **unspent transaction outputs** or **UTXOs**.

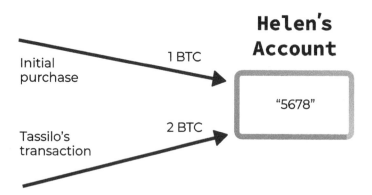

Figure 6.9: Two unspent transaction outputs pointing to Helen's bitcoin address "5678."

Common parlance is to say Helen has three bitcoins in her account. The ledger has a record that one bitcoin is already assigned to Helen's 5678 address that she has not redirected to another address (spent), and it readdresses Tassilos's two bitcoins from his address to Helen's. If Helen wants to check her "account" balance, what she's actually doing is checking how many bitcoins are pointed at her address.

Let's have a closer look at the Tassilo transaction (see Figure 6.10). In Figure 6.9 we saw that one transaction output of 2.0 BTC points to Helen's address, but, as we have discussed before, a transaction can (and often does) have more than one output. In this case the transaction has one input (that is connected to an earlier 9 BTC transaction output) and two outputs (2 BTC to Helen, and 7 BTC to another of Tassilo's addresses). The output to Helen is an unspent transaction output (UTXO), because Helen has not yet spent it, while the transaction output to Tassilo 2 is considered "spent," because Tassilo used the funds in another transaction.

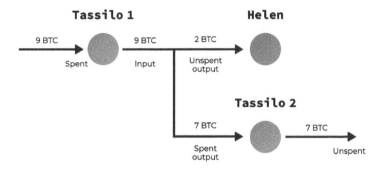

Figure 6.10: Tassilo's transaction: the transaction has one input (9 BTC) and two outputs: one going to Helen's "5678" address, and one going to another address of Tassilo (presumably a change address). Tassilo spent the seven bitcoins from his "Tassilo 2" address in another transaction, while the two bitcoins to Helen are still unspent.

So, internally bitcoin is not aware of "account balances," but is all about connecting arrows with each other, and in particular about keeping track of the arrow outputs that are not pointing anywhere yet (the UTXOs). Only UTXOs can be used in a new transaction, which is why they are so important.

There is one more important rule for connecting arrows: UTXOs have to be fully spent. So in the example (Figure 6.10), Tassilo had to submit a transaction that fully spends the 9 BTC (the output of another transaction), so he (or his software) decided to send 2 BTC to Helen and the remaining 7 BTC to a change address (Tassilo 2).

So bitcoin internally is a mesh of connected arrows with some open ends (the UTXOs), but in most cases it is easier for us to think about it in terms of accounts, and for the rest of this book we'll use this metaphor.

Internally, bitcoin is a mesh of connected arrows that represent transactions. The arrow endings that do not point
anywhere (so called **"unspent transaction output"** or **UTXOs**)
are spendable. For simplicity in everyday use, using the
common account-balance analogy works well.

2.iv. Tainted Coins

Bitcoin transaction histories are recorded in a public database,
and analysis can show that certain bitcoins have in the past
been used for illicit purposes such as illegal drug transactions.
This sort of analysis is done by several specialized companies,
and often accessed by exchanges and other financial service
providers. Coins with a "questionable" history are sometimes
also referred to as "tainted coins."

Please note that there is no standardized definition for a
"tainted" coin. An analysis of any given address will not give
a definitive pass or fail result, but a graded-scale rating, in the
company's judgment, of the address's "purity" or "reputation."
This may differ from company to company. Since this leads
to distinctions between different bitcoins, there are potential consequences for bitcoin's fungibility trait (cf. Chapter
2.2.v), as pure fungibility would imply absolutely no difference
between coins. In a cryptocurrency context, this could only
be achieved by concealing the coin's transactions. As of this
writing, this can't be done with bitcoin, although discussions
continue about the introduction of functionality to enhance
bitcoin transaction privacy.

2.v. Hierarchical Deterministic Wallet

If for every transaction a new change address is generated, the number of addresses a wallet holds can quickly become unwieldy. In 2012 a technique to be used in a type of wallet called a "**hierarchical deterministic wallet**" (or **HD wallet** for short) was implemented to make this process more structured and orderly.

Instead of generating individual private keys separately, first twelve (or twenty-four) words (called **seed words** or **seed**) are chosen from a list of words in a standardized 2048-word dictionary. The private keys in the bitcoin wallet are derived from those twelve words. These seed words can also be stored separately from the wallet as a backup, and are usually stored physically on paper or in metal form so they can be secured (for example in a safe) and are safe from computer hacking, as they are not stored electronically.

3. TYPES OF WALLETS

It is essential to store private keys or seeds safely. Different methods for doing that were invented over time. Each comes with its pros and cons. As of 2021, many people in the industry use hardware wallets that are specifically designed for this purpose, offering a very good compromise between security and usability. However, we will also describe some of the ways that are no longer commonly used for safely storing bitcoin.

Bitcoin wallets are described as **hot** or **cold**. This refers to whether the device used to store the private key is connected to the internet, thus more susceptible to being hacked, or physically air-gapped from the internet. The former is a hot wallet and the latter a cold one. Broadly, there is a tradeoff between security and convenience: hot wallets are easier to use, whereas cold wallets are more secure. A common practice is to keep bitcoins needed for everyday use in a hot wallet, and to have those intended for long-term storage in a cold wallet.

Think of bitcoins as if they were bills. Don't keep more in a hot wallet than you'd carry around with you in cash.

3.i. Paper and Metal Wallets

If Alice writes her private keys down on a piece of paper (and not electronically), she's using a **paper wallet**. Because the private keys are stored offline, they are largely immune from hacker attacks, but the risks are still self-evident. If she forgets where she put the paper, if someone steals it, or it gets wet or catches fire, Alice's paper wallet is destroyed, the private keys on it are irretrievably lost, and the bitcoins stored at the associated address are forever inaccessible. (They are still recorded in the bitcoin ledger though.)

To improve on those weaknesses, there are companies that create fire- and waterproof metal plates that can be engraved either with the private key itself, or with the seed words that can be used to generate the private keys.

3.ii. Hardware Wallets

Private keys or seeds can be stored in a hardware wallet, a small computer peripheral, which looks similar to a USB stick and can be attached to a PC when access to the wallet is required. Typically, these auto-generate a sequence of twenty-four random words (the seed), which can be used to recover the keys if the device is destroyed or lost.

In addition, a PIN number is set by the user, which needs to be entered to use the device, offering protection against accessing the device if it is stolen.

Having something tangible can sometimes create confusion. A hardware wallet doesn't store bitcoins on the thumb drive or USB stick, but rather the private keys that allow the user to access the bitcoins. The bitcoins themselves are stored on each node of the bitcoin network (cf. Chapter 6.1.ii "The Bitcoin Ledger"), and thus are not affected by the method of storing the private keys.

It is normally fine if the hardware wallet is lost or destroyed, as long as the seed phrase has been stored in a safe place. If, however, the piece of hardware is the only place the private keys to those bitcoins are recorded, they are now inaccessible.

3.iii. Software Wallet on Computer (Online/Offline)

A software wallet on a computer can be as simple (and foolhardy) as a text file stored on your computer or a cloud service like Dropbox into which you copy-paste your private keys.

To get around the problem of keeping digitally stored private keys safe from hackers, some people keep their digital wallets on what are called **air-gapped** or **offline** computers. These are machines not connected to the internet in any way, so that information kept there and nowhere else is reasonably secure against hacker attacks, although still vulnerable to hard drive failure or theft.

3.iv. Mobile Phone Wallet

A mobile phone can also be used to store bitcoin. Many apps exist with the same functionality as wallet software for PCs, and this makes it convenient to carry around, so that bitcoin can be used for retail transactions. Since mobile phones are generally connected to the internet, these are vulnerable to hacking, and so are only recommended for small amounts for everyday use and not for the storage of large amounts of bitcoin.

3.v. Online Wallet

Online wallets are a service offered by a number of providers that offer the "secure" storage of private keys. The bitcoins can be stored, sent, and received using the website or app the service provides. It is important to note that no matter what these services guarantee or how ironclad their contracts are, ultimately, if you are not in sole control of your private keys, you are not in control of your cryptocurrency.

Exchanges also, either as an extra service or as de facto practice, have wallet functionality. But as with all other types of online wallet, the private keys are not held by the user and are therefore not recommended for long-term bitcoin holdings.

3.vi. Brain Wallets

If Alice memorizes her private keys or the seed words that can generate the private keys, she's using a "brain wallet." The drawbacks here are obvious. If she forgets or transposes even a single digit or word (or if she dies), her bitcoins are forever inaccessible.[66]

3.vii. Summary

Paper and metal wallets are cumbersome to create, and difficult to use. You also need to be careful that the chosen password is sufficiently random and secure. Brain wallets are dangerous in the sense that you can lose everything. Don't use them unless you have to.

For smaller amounts and for testing purposes it makes perfect sense to use a software wallet on your mobile or computer, or a hosted web wallet. However, for larger amounts we strongly recommend using a hardware wallet, which combines high security with good usability.

The following scores are to a certain degree subjective, but will give you an indication on the security/usage tradeoffs for the different solutions.

---

66 Some services offer to brute-force a seed or password if you at least know most of it. There is no guarantee this will work, and you also have to trust the service provider.

Wallet Security Comparison

Device	Security	Usage	Hot / Cold
Paper Wallet	+ / ++	—	cold
Metal Wallet	++	—	cold
Hardware Wallet	++	+	cold*
Software (Online)	O	++	hot
Software (Offline)	+ / ++	O	hot
Mobile Wallet	O	++	hot
Browser Wallet	O**	+ / ++	hot
Brain Wallet	++	-	cold

(*) Access to the hardware device occurs via a USB cable. While there is no air-gap between the computer and the hardware wallet, we are also not aware of any security issues with the USB connection, and thus consider hardware wallets to be "cold."

(**) depending on the security of the wallet provider

Figure 6.11: Comparison of the security of bitcoin wallets

4. ACQUIRING BITCOIN

Once you have a wallet that allows you to create addresses and their associated private keys, and also have a way of safely storing those keys, there are two ways to fill it with bitcoin: buy it (exchange fiat money for bitcoin) or mine it. We'll cover bitcoin mining in the next section, focusing first on the ways fiat currency is exchanged for bitcoin.

Bitcoin exchanges are the gateways between the fiat and cryptocurrency worlds. Because bitcoin is both a currency and a payment system, these exchanges are not entirely analogous to the currency-exchange kiosks found in airports where, for example, American passengers might exchange the US dollars in their wallets for euros. Rather, bitcoin exchanges are better thought of as the points of contact between the global fiat banking system and the bitcoin network.

4.i. Cryptocurrency Exchanges

Security

One of the biggest risks that a user of an exchange faces is if the exchange disappears or goes bankrupt, or its funds are stolen. The user then faces losing some or all of the bitcoin and/or fiat currency held on the exchange. Many cases of this have occurred during the history of bitcoin, from exchanges having large amounts of cryptocurrency stolen, to the exchange itself being a scam and the operators disappearing with the funds held. For this reason, it is advantageous for the user if the exchange is regulated by state authorities, as conventional financial institutions are, because this adds an extra layer of professional scrutiny to reduce the chance of fraud or theft occurring.

The second security risk users encounter lies in the account itself. Even if the exchange is trustworthy and well managed, with excellent protection against theft, the user still faces the danger that someone could access the exchange account without authorization, just like someone could take the password to an email account or bank account and use it to get access. Someone with unauthorized access to an exchange account could steal the bitcoin or fiat currency held in it, or make transactions without permission.[67] Two factor authentication ("2FA") is one frequently used security measure at bitcoin exchanges, where the user must complete two separate stages in proving identity, such as a password and a security code.

Reputable exchanges perform checks whether the bitcoins being deposited are tainted, and in case of doubt will question the sender. They can even freeze bitcoins with a questionable background. This means that the coins that the exchange possesses, and later sends to users requesting withdrawals, will have passed their check procedure, providing some protection for the exchange user against receiving bitcoins with a dubious past.

---

67   While it is usually difficult to steal fiat money from an exchange account (wire transfers often are reversible for a certain period of time), most attackers will convert the fiat money to bitcoin (or another cryptocurrency) and withdraw the coins to one of their addresses—a process that, in the case of bitcoin, is irreversible.

4.ii. Other Means of Acquiring Bitcoin

Bitcoin ATM

If Alice had the $100 she'd earmarked for buying bitcoin in cash for some reason, she wouldn't have to involve a bank at all. She could bring the bills to a bitcoin ATM, which, similarly to a regular ATM, allows her to deposit her money. However, instead of crediting the money to her fiat account, the bitcoin ATM would convert it into bitcoin, and send the bitcoins she received to her wallet's address. Therefore, Bitcoin ATMs are the physical world's approximation of a bitcoin exchange.

Please note:

- For providing this service the ATM provider typically charges a fee of 8–10 percent, so ATMs are a rather expensive way of acquiring bitcoin.

- The bitcoins should be moved from the paper wallet provided by the ATM to a wallet created by the purchaser, as the purchaser cannot be sure that no one else has the private key provided by the ATM.

- In several jurisdictions, ATMs require a scan of an ID or passport to check the user's identity.

Some ATMs also conduct the reverse transaction, i.e., providing fiat money in return for bitcoin. If Alice has bitcoins in her wallet and wants cash, she can send bitcoins from her wallet to the ATM and take bills out of the machine. In either instance, the biggest difference for Alice between this and depositing or withdrawing cash from a checking account is that she uses a phone app rather than a plastic card and ATM keypad to "talk" to the machine, which still accepts or dispenses cash in the traditional way.

There are bitcoin ATMs all over the world with new ones being added frequently. They can be found through ATM search websites, and most readers will likely find one within a reasonable distance.

In Person

In the first few years after bitcoin started, it was difficult to obtain, as only very few exchanges existed, and these were not easily accessible. Therefore, a common means of acquiring small amounts of bitcoin was to meet directly with people who had some and to buy coins from them. As bitcoin transactions are irreversible, an in-person meeting was considered the safest method of exchanging cash for bitcoin.

Since it is not always possible to verify the identity and background of both parties, and there being no straightforward way to check in advance that the coins are not tainted, this is not the safest way to purchase bitcoin. Fraud has occurred in the course of such transactions. The simple possibility of the cash simply being stolen can't be ruled out. With the rise in the accessibility and regulation of cryptocurrency exchanges in many areas, this method of purchasing bitcoins has been eclipsed, though it is still relevant in places with a poor exchange infrastructure.

If Alice's friend Bob is already into bitcoin, she might arrange to meet him somewhere. They would agree on a price, Alice would give Bob the cash and the address of her bitcoin wallet, and he would use an app on his phone to initiate a transaction, transferring the agreed-upon amount of bitcoin to her.

If Alice doesn't know anyone willing to sell her bitcoin in person, she can go to a peer-to-peer marketplace. On a peer-to-peer marketplace, private individuals list offers to buy and sell bitcoin, and then conduct the transaction directly, that is, peer-to-peer, between themselves, either by meeting in person and exchanging bitcoin for cash, or remotely with a bank transfer or other electronic means being used to exchange the fiat currency.

There is an important distinction between this and a bitcoin exchange, which has major legal implications:

- Buying on an exchange means that your contract party is the exchange, and in case something goes wrong, the company can be held accountable.

- When buying from another person (whom you found at the peer-to-peer marketplace), this other person is your contract party (and not the peer-to-peer market- place). In many cases neither the p2p marketplace nor you will know your counterparty's identity.

Since the parties do not know each other, both sides have the risk of the uncertainty that the other party will fulfill their side of the agreement. Although this can be mitigated by using an escrow account, there would still be the difficulty of proving any claim to the escrow service provider. If meeting in person in a non-public location, the physical security issue of being threatened is also a concern.

5. MINING AND ACHIEVING CONSENSUS

In the beginning of this chapter we talked about bitcoin transactions but did not explain how the actual processing of a transaction works. This is where bitcoin mining comes into play. It might look like an unnecessary feature at the beginning, but in fact bitcoin mining is a fundamental part of the system that ensures:

1. reaching consensus among all participating nodes in a distributed system, and

2. distributing newly generated bitcoins to participants.

We'll begin by explaining the properties of bitcoin mining, without losing ourselves in the technical details. This way you can get a good conceptual understanding of what mining is and how the economics of bitcoin mining work. This will enable you to understand 99 percent of all mining-related discussions. In Chapter 8 of the book we will go one step further and explain the details of the mining process. Understanding mining is needed to fully appreciate how consensus is achieved, that is, how a network of decentralized nodes reaches agreement on the new entries in the ledger, without having a centralized authority determine this.

Achieving consensus means that all nodes of a network are in agreement about something, e.g., whether a transaction should be processed or not. Reaching consensus in a centralized system is relatively easy to achieve, while it is difficult in a decentralized system.

A set of rules and procedures that leads to consensus is referred to as a **consensus algorithm** or **consensus mechanism**.

5.i. Transaction Processing in a Centralized System

Before examining how transactions are processed in a decentralized system, let us for comparison describe the situation for a centralized system. There, updating a ledger of transactions is organized by one single authority (the "central node"). In this case, a transaction becomes valid if the central authority accepts it on its ledger, and all other participants will refer to that central authority in order to check whether a transaction is valid or not.

For example, Alice, who is connected to "node 1," wants to send 1 USD to Bob (see Figure 6.12). Then "node 1" will send the transaction to the "central node," which will decide whether the transaction is valid or not. If it is accepted by the central node, its ledger will be updated accordingly, and the other nodes 2–5 will get an update from the "central node."

There is also the necessity to reject fraudulent transaction attempts should they occur. In the double-spend problem, a participant deceitfully tries to spend the same money twice. We discussed double spends in Chapter 1.2.iii. Two contradictory transactions are sent to the system, and for the system to maintain its integrity, at least one of the transactions must be rejected.

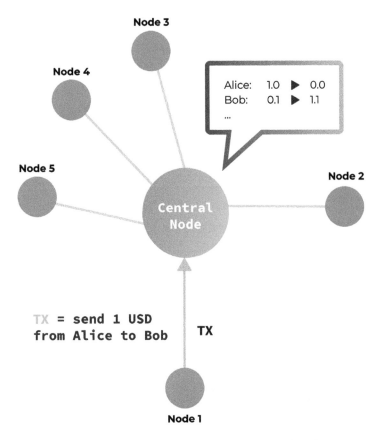

Figure 6.12: Alice sends 1 USD to Bob in a centralized system.

In a centralized system, a decision is taken by a single central authority, which will recognize what has happened and decide either to accept one transaction as valid and reject the other, or recognize the fraudulent double-spend attempt and reject both transactions. All other participants in the network can then refer to the decision made by the central authority. In this way, a consensus in the network is achieved by one party, which is then accepted by everyone else.

5.ii. Achieving Consensus in a Decentralized System Is Difficult

One could expect that in a decentralized system the participating nodes also just update their respective ledger when they get notice of a new transaction, but as we will see, it is not so simple.

In the following example (Figure 6.13), the node at the bottom generates a transaction ("send 1 bitcoin from Alice to Bob"), updates its own ledger, and informs its two neighbors about the transaction. We will denote the nodes which receive the transaction to Bob first, as "B" nodes.

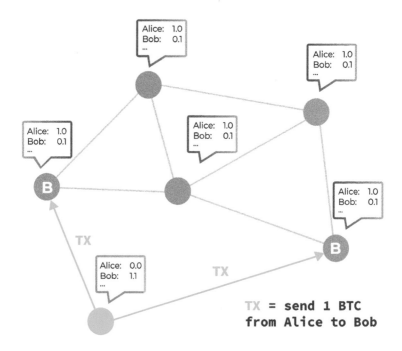

Figure 6.13: Alice sends 1 BTC to Bob in a decentralized system.

The two receiving nodes will update their ledger too, and pass the information about the transaction on to their neighbors in turn (see Figure 6.14).

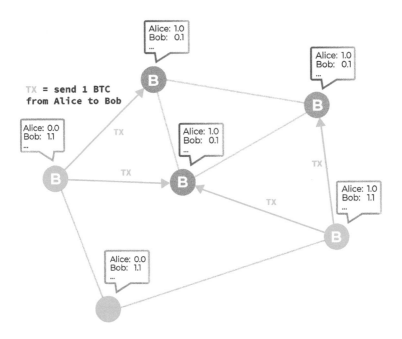

Figure 6.14: Alice's transaction to Bob is propagated through the decentralized system.

This process of transaction propagation iterates until all nodes in the network have been informed about the transaction. On completion, the ledger entries of every node will be consistent. Most transactions will normally be carried out by honest actors and be undisputed. If all transactions were like that, the above system would be sufficient.

However, the system must also handle the double-spend problem, i.e., it must maintain its integrity if two contradictory transactions are sent to the system. For example, in Figure 6.15 we see that one node simultaneously sends two inconsistent transactions:

1. one transaction, "send one bitcoin from Alice to Bob," is sent to one node, and

2. the other transaction, "send one bitcoin from Alice to Charlie," is sent to another node.

We will denote the node which receives the transaction to Bob first as the "B" node, and the node receiving the transaction to Charlie first as the "C" node.

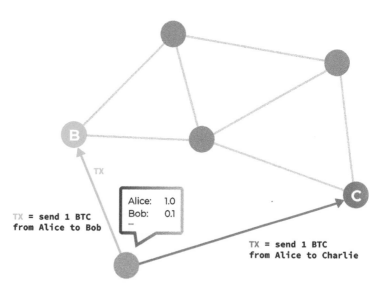

Figure 6.15: A transaction from Alice to Bob is sent to one node, but a conflicting transaction from Alice to Charlie is sent to another node.

The transactions are inconsistent because Alice only has one bitcoin. Seen separately, both transactions are correct, but both transactions cannot simultaneously be honest. The net result of sending two transactions, in each of which she spends one bitcoin, is that she is spending—or attempting to spend— two bitcoins when she only has one.

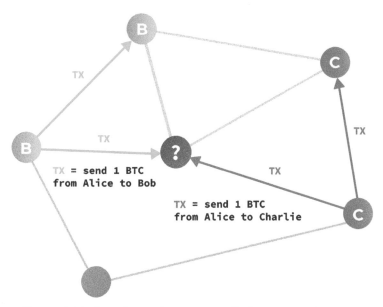

Figure 6.16: A node receives two conflicting transactions.

In Figure 6.15 the situation arises that the "B" node and the "C" node have ledgers different from each other. If both nodes continue to propagate the transaction (as in Figure 6.14), the conflict will be even more obvious (cf. Figure 6.16): the node in the middle realizes there is a conflict and cannot decide how to update its ledger. In this case, the desired outcome of all ledger copies being in agreement is not satisfied. To simply accept the first transaction received and reject any subsequent contradictory transactions does not work, because there is no way to ensure that all nodes receive transactions in the same order in time.

This example shows the shortcomings of using a straightforward system to maintain the consistency of ledger copies in a decentralized network. A dishonest actor can easily cause the failure of the system by providing different nodes with conflicting inputs, and the system lacks a way to resolve them. Therefore, a different consensus mechanism is required, which we will discuss in the next section, and in more detail in Chapter 8.3.

To recap: with a central authority in place, the double-spend problem can be solved, because the central authority can order events in time (this is called **time-ordering**). It knows whether Bob or Charlie came in first to redeem their check (cf. Chapter 1.2.iii). However, in the decentralized world, this isn't possible. Different nodes will hear about the existence of the Bob and Charlie transactions at different times. Some nodes will receive the Bob transaction first and the Charlie transaction second, and vice versa. In this case it is not possible to time-order the events.

5.iii. Blocks and Bitcoin Mining

As explained above, the decentralized nature of bitcoin means that there cannot be a central instance that decides which transactions should be accepted by all participants to update their (local) bitcoin ledger. Instead there is a group of special bitcoin nodes (called **miners** or **mining nodes**) that is vital for reaching consensus. In simplified terms, there is a process that allows mining nodes to take turns confirming transactions, which then will be accepted by all nodes to update their own copy of the bitcoin ledger. After the update, all nodes will have the same account balances, and consensus is achieved.

For reasons we will learn later, bitcoin transactions are bundled together in groups that are called **blocks**. These blocks are an important part of a structure called the **blockchain**, which we will study in detail in Chapter 8.3. For now, it is sufficient to simply think of a block as a "group of transactions."

Mining nodes create (or produce) new blocks, which means that they select a group of unconfirmed transactions with the intent that these transactions (the block) will be accepted by all other nodes. In order to produce a valid new block accepted by the other nodes, mining nodes have to solve a very complicated mathematical problem. The mining node that solves the problem first can circulate a new block, which also includes the solution for the mathematical problem, to the rest of the network. The nature of the mathematical problem is such that it is very hard to solve, but once a solution has been found it is very easy to verify that the solution is indeed correct. This can be compared with a combination lock: if a lock has four digits, it takes a long time to try all the possible combinations, but a proposed solution can be easily checked simply by confirming that the solution does in fact open the lock.

Many different terms are used to describe the process of selecting transactions, forming a block, and solving the complicated mathematical problem: **creating**, **producing**, **solving**, **finding**, and **mining a block** are all used synonymously.

The miner must expend considerable computational power in order to find a solution, requiring expenditure on specialized mining computers, cooling equipment for the computers, ancillary hardware such as power supplies, and the electricity to run them. So that the miner has an economic incentive to undertake these costs, a reward, which has two components, is given to the miner who successfully finds a new block. The reward's first component is the new bitcoins generated as part of the new block (also called the **block reward**). This is important since this is the only way that new bitcoins are created.

The second component is through transaction fees (which we looked into in Chapter 5.3.ii). In every transaction the sender chooses a transaction fee, which incentivizes the miner to include that transaction in a transaction block. For example, let's assume Alice is willing to pay 2 mBTC (one mBTC is a thousandth of a bitcoin), Bob is offering 3 mBTC, and Charlie 1 mBTC, and that a block can only hold two transactions. A profit-maximizing miner would obviously include Alice's and Bob's transaction, and Charlie would have to hope—but is not guaranteed—that his transaction is processed in one of the following blocks.[68] If Charlie's fee is too low, Charlie's transaction may never be included in any block. In the bitcoin network practically all miners optimize for profit, and thus will include the transactions offering the highest fees.

Important to note is the analogy between bitcoin mining and mining for physical resources such as gold. Just as a gold miner must expend physical energy in order to extract gold,

---

68 The transaction fees and block size are for illustrative purposes only, i.e., the real number of transactions that fit into one block is in the thousands.

a bitcoin miner takes a real-world physical resource—electrical energy—as an input to generate new bitcoins, received as part of the block reward. In this way, unlike a digital currency created by an entry in a database, there is a necessary and direct link between a hard physical input in the form of electrical energy and the creation of new bitcoins. Or otherwise phrased, in order to generate new bitcoins, a real-world, physical, and thus scarce input in the form of a large quantity of electricity is required. This is the reason it is called mining, because, as with gold or coal mining, energy is used to extract a precious resource. For this reason, analogous terminology taken from traditional mining is also used in bitcoin mining.

If a miner has solved the hard mathematical problem, we say in bitcoin terminology that the miner has **solved a block** or **mined a block** or **produced a block**. Transactions included in such a newly produced block are considered (in almost all cases) to be "confirmed." We will discuss the exceptions in more detail in Chapter 8.3.ii. For now it is sufficient to assume that all transactions in a solved block are confirmed, which means that all nodes will use the confirmed transactions to update their (local) ledgers.

Summary:

- Transactions are processed in groups called "blocks."

- Miners are special bitcoin nodes that solve computationally difficult problems.

- By doing so, they produce blocks of confirmed transactions that other nodes will use to update their ledger.

- Miners get a reward for solving blocks (new bitcoins and fees from the transactions that are part of the block).

- Miners are essential to keep bitcoin secure and decentralized.

5.iv. The Bitcoin Node Network

The bitcoin network is designed to be decentralized and peer-to-peer, where everyone can take a part in it without anyone's permission (this property is also referred to as **permission-less**). A **node** is simply the bitcoin software running on a computer, which means it follows certain rules and shares information. Nodes connect over the internet to other nodes and thus form the **bitcoin node network**. Each node will independently verify all transactions and blocks it receives; they are gatekeepers that filter out malicious transactions and blocks (e.g., double-spending attempts).

A bitcoin node usually refers to a **full node**, which is characterized as follows:

- It holds a complete history of all blocks since its inception, thus maintaining the bitcoin ledger.

- When a full node starts for the first time, it starts to download all blocks (beginning with the first block) from its peers.

- It will validate all blocks and transactions, beginning with the very first transaction made with bitcoin back in 2009, and does so for every transaction up to the present. In this way, it does not rely on or trust any third party that any transaction in the bitcoin ledger is valid, but rather checks each and every single transaction for itself.

- It checks and relays unconfirmed transactions to other peers.

- It will share its copy of blocks to other nodes if requested.

A **mining node**, a node that can produce a new block, must be a full node. Other types of nodes exist, e.g., "light nodes," but for now it is sufficient to imagine that all nodes in the bitcoin node network are mining or full nodes.

The more bitcoin nodes that are running and connected to the rest of the network, the higher the degree of decentralization, promoting the positive consequences of decentralization, such as robustness and its permissionless nature. If some of the bitcoin nodes (full nodes or mining nodes) disappeared from one second to the next, the remaining nodes would still do the job of validating and processing transactions, and the bitcoin system would continue without interruption. The property of withstanding even major damage (like a loss of a large number of nodes) is referred to as **resilience**. Bitcoin node software is available for all modern operating systems (such as Windows, macOS, or Linux) available today and can be freely downloaded and used without any restrictions. The requirements for running a full node are standard computer hardware and a reliable internet connection, and therefore, since these requirements are quite low, many are able to run a bitcoin node.

In the same way that streets are the main component of infrastructure for cars, trucks, and buses, the bitcoin node network forms the backbone of the infrastructure for bitcoin wallet clients and miners.

CHAPTER SUMMARY

Private keys are needed in order to access and transfer bitcoins, and must be protected at all times to ensure the safety of users' bitcoins. Bitcoin wallets allow users to manage those private keys, and hardware wallets offer a good combination of security and convenience. Cryptocurrency exchanges are the most common way to acquire or dispose of bitcoins. The current status of all transactions is tracked by the global bitcoin ledger, a copy of which is stored on every node. An integral part of ensuring that all the copies of the bitcoin ledger remain in agreement in bitcoin's decentralized system is an energy- and cost-intensive system called mining, which gathers a number of transactions together into a structure referred to as a block.

7

CRYPTOGRAPHIC PRIMITIVES

IN THE 1999 FILM *THE MATRIX*, NEO WAKES UP TO HIS COMPUTER directing him to: "Follow the white rabbit." He does and ends up meeting a character who offers him a choice of pills. If he takes the red one, he's told, he will stay in Wonderland and learn "how deep the rabbit hole goes."

The bitcoin rabbit hole goes very deep. We have worked excessively long hours every day for ten years and haven't plumbed its depths yet, so what we offer in the next two chapters is maybe half a red pill.

Shifting metaphorical gears, if we're driving, not diving, the previous chapter provided what we hope is a useful driving manual while the ones before it explained how and why a car operates the way it does. To better understand its operation, this chapter disassembles the vehicle. We've talked about bitcoin accounts and private keys, but there are no accounts and no locks (and no spoon). Let's take a half pill and see how it works.

Cryptographic Primitives are well-established, elementary
cryptographic algorithms that are often used in cryptographic
protocols. This means that for decades, these algorithms
could not be broken by the cryptographic community, important for building a secure system.

1. CRYPTOGRAPHIC HASH FUNCTIONS

Every digital property—every text file, video, picture, or
computer program—is, at the most granular level, just a very
(very) long list of ones and zeros. Imagine Alice, for example, has just downloaded ten gigabytes of research data from
a colleague, Bob. Because the accuracy of her work depends
on this information being exactly correct, and because files
can be corrupted through uploading and downloading, she
wants to make sure hers is a complete and accurate copy of the
original. She could, in theory, download the entire file again
and compare the two copies. It would be a bit like mapping a
person's entire genome first today and then tomorrow to verify
they haven't changed overnight. However, once the comparison was complete, if Alice's two copies are identical, she could
be reasonably confident her download was good, since it's
unlikely that two downloads would contain the same error.

On the other hand, if Alice's downloaded files differ, one or
both might be bad copies, and she wouldn't know which.

Cryptographic hash functions (or just **hash functions**)
are a bit like fingerprint-making machines. They produce a
compact identifier (called a **digest** or **hash**) whose relationship

to input data is like that of fingerprint to person. Because the complex mathematics of hash functions is beyond the scope of our rabbit hole, they're best thought of as black boxes that accept inputs and produce outputs.[69]

1.i. Properties

To return to our example, Bob would feed his ten gigabytes of ones and zeros into this machine, and it would output a hash that's small and compact enough for easy one-to-one comparison. Alice would then download the data and apply the same hash function. Different types of hash functions exist, the most important to bitcoin being SHA-2.[70] (SHA stands for Secure Hashing Algorithm.) Because the resultant hash is mathematically generated by using each and every zero and one in the file, if Alice's hash matches Bob's, they can be certain they have identical data.[71] This certainty derives from the three critical properties of cryptographic hash functions, which also make them integral to bitcoin. Cryptographic hashes usually have the following properties:

---

69 In science, computing, and engineering, a black box is a device, system, or object that can be used effectively without any knowledge of its internal workings. An example could be an iPhone: not knowing how it works doesn't impede the ability to make calls, take pictures, or otherwise operate the phone. That said, bitcoin is open protocol and open source, so, unlike a phone, anyone who wants to can open the hash-function black box, see precisely how the math works, and replicate it themselves.

70 Pronounced "sha." In bitcoin literature, there are also often references to SHA-256; for all intents and purposes, these are the same.

71 In practice, this is certain because the probability of finding a collision among a billion hashes is 1 in 4.3×10^{-60}, and thus, it is orders of magnitude less likely than the earth being hit by a "killer" asteroid.

- They are deterministic.

- Small changes in the input cause huge change in the hash ("avalanche effect").

- They are generally quick to compute.

- They are unidirectional.

Finally, the output always has the same length. Regardless of whether the input to the hash function is a single letter, a short phrase, or, as in the example above, a 10 gigabyte file, the output will always be the same length.

A few examples are shown in Figure 7.1.

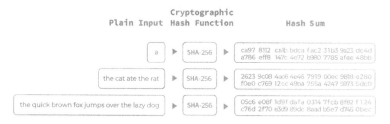

Figure 7.1: Examples of SHA-256 outputs for various inputs. Notice that the output always has the same length: 256 bits, hence SHA-256.

Deterministic

Being deterministic means the same input always yields the same output. To use the example above, the text "the cat ate the rat" run through a SHA-2 hash function always generates the string of numbers and letters on the right beginning with 2623 9c08 and ending with 5dc0. Put another way, 2623 9c08 ... is and will always be the only SHA-2 hash of "the cat ate the rat." Likewise, when Alice runs the entire ten gigabytes of Bob's data, the hash she gets will be the same as Bob's if her download is identical to his. There is nothing random or arbitrary in the hash, and even after a thousand times or in a hundred years, the same file will yield the same hash.

> The same data run through the same hash function always produces the same hash.

Avalanche Effect

In the example below you will notice that a small change in the input from "rat" to "bat" results in a completely different hash value. The first hash value seems to be uncorrelated with the second, although the inputs were very similar. This property of a hash function, that small changes in the input result in big changes in the output, is referred to as "avalanche effect."

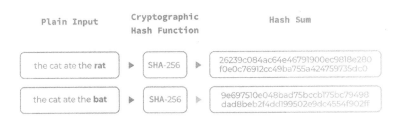

Figure 7.2: SHA-256 inputs and outputs: a small difference in input results in a large difference in output.

Because even a minimal change in the input disproportionally changes the output, hash functions make it very easy to see not *how* inputs are different, but *that* they are. Given the hash of "the cat ate the rat" is always 2623 9c08 4ac6 ..., if the hash of "the cat ate the bat" were 2623 9c08 4bc6 ..., the function would be less useful than the actual hash of "the cat ate the bat," which begins with 9e69 7510 e048 ...

Quick to Compute

In general it is helpful if a hash can be generated very quickly and does not require too many computational resources. For example, you could run a hash function over a million different files in a storage system in order to determine which are duplicates of others, a process that you would prefer not to take a long time.

While most hash functions are designed to be easy to compute, there are also some, e.g., the "scrypt" hash function, that make it intentionally hard to calculate a hash.[72]

Unidirectional

Particularly because they're often used for security, it's critical that while the hash of a file (or of a password or a private key) is determined by its contents, it's not possible to arrive at the contents by knowing the hash. There is no known way to "reverse" a hash function. While it is very easy to calculate

---

72 This is mainly done to slow down brute-force attempts for cracking passwords.

the hash of an input, the opposite (finding an input for a given hash) is impossible.

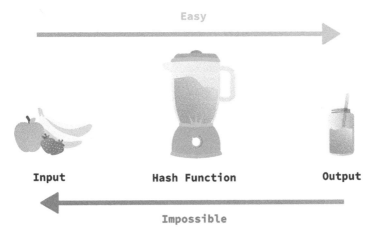

Figure 7.3: Hash functions are one-way functions. (Source: "One Way Function," Computer Science Wiki, last modified March 8, 2020, https://computersciencewiki.org/index.php/File:One_way_function.png.)

A mathematical function that is easy in one direction and very difficult in the opposite direction is also called a **one-way function**.

There is no way to arrive at "the cat ate the rat" from the 2623 9c08 ... hash. Additionally, 2623 9c08 ... might be the hash of several other sentences, none of which have anything to do with cats, rats, and eating.[73]

---

73 Most likely, a text that results in the same hash will look like a random sequence of characters (e.g., "Asfp!Oie_fa$FE") rather than an actual sentence.

1.ii. Applications

Being deterministic and unidirectional, and having the "avalanche effect," makes hash functions useful for a variety of applications. The easiest to use as an example (and by far the most common) is the storage of passwords, but there are many bitcoin-specific applications as well.

Satoshi made heavy use of cryptographic hash functions in the bitcoin protocol. For example, they are used in a part of bitcoin called "proof of work," which protects the integrity of the ledger. Furthermore, hash functions are used in the formation of bitcoin addresses. In order to better understand how hash functions can be used to solve real problems, we'll look first at password storage, reserving more complex bitcoin applications for the next chapter.

Password Storage

Websites for everything from banks to bookstores require users to sign in with a password. Alice of course expects that if she enters her username and password, she will be able to log in to Bob's website. But how does his website ensure that Alice has entered the correct password? The simple way (which was used for a long time in the early days of the internet) is for Bob just to store the plain password in a database. The database would contain all usernames and their respective passwords. However, this turned out to be a severe security risk! If Craig manages to "hack" the website he would gain access to the plain list of all passwords of Bob's clients. As it is a burden to generate and keep track of many different passwords, many users reuse a password on other websites, thus allowing Craig to hack into many more accounts on other websites.

A safer alternative to storing the plain password is to store its hash. When Alice enters her password, Bob's website runs what she's entered through the hash function black box. Because hash functions are deterministic, if the result matches what the website has on file, he can be reasonably confident that the user on the other end is, in fact, Alice.

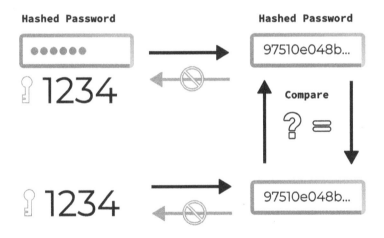

Figure 7.4: The hashes of passwords are compared for authentication.

If Craig hacks Bob's website, he will now only obtain a list of hashes (of passwords), but not the passwords themselves. As the hash function is unidirectional, Craig can't derive the password from its hash. For the same reason, if Alice loses her password, the website can't email it to her because all it has is its hash. This is the reason why websites will ask you to create a new password instead of sending you your old one. If a website ever sends you back your old password, it means that they are not taking your security seriously.

Bitcoin Addresses and Fingerprints

Cryptographic hash functions can also be used to protect users from mistyping a bitcoin address, by adding a "fingerprint" to the address. How does it work?

If Alice sends a letter to Bob that contains the string "ABCD" and her handwriting is not very clear, there is a risk that Bob mistakenly reads the "B" as "8" and thinks the string in fact is "A8CD." With longer combinations, e.g., a bank account number that contains many zeros, there is the risk that the receiver mistypes the number, too.

To add extra safety Alice can calculate the SHA-2 hash of the string she wants to send, e.g.,

SHA-2("ABCD") = "e12e 115a cf45 52b2 568b... 7faf c997 882a 02d2 3677"

Alice could add the whole hash to the letter, which would allow Bob to check for himself whether "A8CD" is the correct reading of the text.[74] If it is not, he can at least ask Alice to send it again. In most situations correct spelling might not be important. However, when it comes to sending 1,000 bitcoins to a

---

74 Bob might correctly read the text as "ABCD" but mistype the hash, in which case he would contact Alice again and ask her to resend the letter.

bitcoin address, you want to be 100 percent certain that you are sending it to the right recipient.

Adding the hash to the text provides this extra security. However, it also results in adding a lot of extra characters to the rather short text "ABCD." Instead of adding the whole hash to the actual text, bitcoin addresses only use the first four bytes of the hash.

> A **byte** is a very common unit of digital information, consisting of eight bits, which is enough to represent the decimal numbers from 0 to 255. The size of files and apps is typically measured in Mega- or Gigabytes.

In the following, we simplify a little bit for illustrational purposes and assume that "ABCD" is the "raw" bitcoin address and that "e12e 115a" represents the four first bytes of the hash.[75] Adding the last eight characters to the "raw" bitcoin address results in:

bitcoin address = ABCD e12e 115a (fictional example)

The last four bytes (=8 characters) are referred to as the **fingerprint**, and adding those reduces the chance of mistyping a bitcoin address to about one in four billion. The fingerprint is part of every bitcoin address, so if someone sends you a bitcoin address, this type of error detection is already integrated in the

---

75   Two characters represent one byte. For example, "e1" represents the decimal number 225, "2e" represents the number 46, and so on. This is called a "hexadecimal" representation. Thus, "e12e 115a" is a representation for the first four bytes.

address. Importantly, this process doesn't correct any errors it finds, it merely rejects the address that contains them.

> The output of a hashing function can be used to verify data integrity. It is often referred to as a **hash**, **fingerprint**, or **checksum**.

2. PUBLIC-KEY CRYPTOGRAPHY

In the previous section we showed how a hash function can be used to make bitcoin address usage safer, and also hinted that they also play an important role in bitcoin mining. One very important aspect is that of digital ownership. How can Alice prove that she is the owner of the bitcoin that is in the bitcoin address she claims? And how can the bitcoin network determine that Bob cannot spend Alice's bitcoin? Public-key cryptography and digital signatures hold the key to solving this issue.

2.i. Secure Communication

The concept of **public-key cryptography** (or **asymmetric cryptography**) was developed more than fifty years ago, and it has been proven to withstand all attempts to break it.[76] Various

---

76 RSA is a public-key system that uses prime numbers and was developed by Ron Rivest, Adi Shamir, and Leonard Adleman in 1977. Clifford Cocks found a similar system in 1973, but GCHQ (the UK equivalent of the NSA) only declassified his findings in 1997. Another important work was the Diffie-Hellman key exchange (published 1976), which is a method to exchange cryptographic keys securely over a public channel. The protocol is named after Whitfield Diffie and Martin Hellman.

mathematical implementations of public-key cryptography exist. They all use a mathematical one-way function, which we discussed in Chapter 7.1.i.

Asymmetric encryption is easiest to understand in contrast to the older, symmetric forms of encryption. As an example, if Alice and Bob communicate using a simple Caesar cipher, she creates a coded message by shifting each letter up (or backward) along the alphabet by three places, such that ABC becomes XYZ and "hi" is written "ef." Because Bob also needs to know which cipher they're using and how it is decoded, it's said to be symmetrical. There is one code or "key" to lock and unlock the cipher. These are the kind of encryptions that give rise to closely guarded codebooks and enigma machines. Crackers break symmetric codes by figuring out the formula for encoding (and therefore decoding) them because that formula is the same for both and works in opposite directions. Asymmetric codes, in contrast, work in only one direction (they're unidirectional) and require two keys (one for encryption and another for decryption).

Symmetric Cryptography is a cryptography that uses the same cryptographic key for encryption and decryption.

Asymmetric Cryptography is a cryptography that uses different cryptographic keys for encryption and decryption.

Symmetric Encryption

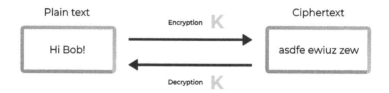

Asymmetric Encryption

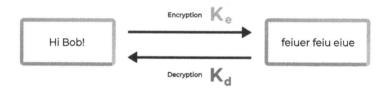

Figure 7.5: Symmetric encryption uses only one key, while asymmetric encryption has different keys for encryption and decryption.

The difference between symmetric and asymmetric might seem like a minor technical detail, but its implications are huge. When using symmetric encryption the receiver must somehow get the secret key from the sender. With asymmetric encryption there is no such restriction, and thus users never have to reveal their private keys. As private keys determine bitcoin ownership, this is very important.

Like the cryptographic hash function, encryption is a one-way function. The ciphertext can be generated quickly, but there is no known way to get the plaintext back from a ciphertext. To understand how this works, we'll take factorization as a (relatively) simple example.

If Alice multiplies the two prime numbers three and seven (3 × 7) and sends Bob the result, twenty-one (21), she could tell him that she reached her result by multiplying prime numbers. Because these are small numbers, Bob wouldn't have any trouble figuring out she'd multiplied three and seven. If, however, she sent him the number 2627 and told him she reached it by multiplying primes, it would take him much longer to arrive at 37 × 71. Because it's much faster for Alice to do the multiplication than it is for Bob to undo it, factorization is a one-way function. If the number Alice sends Bob is over a hundred digits long, it would be effectively impossible for him to decode it. Knowing Alice's method—multiplying primes—doesn't break her code the way knowing Caesar's method—shifting letters—does.

In a very simplified example, this unidirectionality can be used to create an asymmetrical, two-key lock. Imagine Alice goes to the post office and rents a mailbox, which comes with lock 2627.[77] Alice gets two keys for that lock, a public and a private one, 71 and 37. Alice can tell Bob her public key (71), with which Bob can "open" Alice's incoming mailbox, but is only able to leave something in it. Only Alice, using her private key (37), can take things out of it.

---

77 This extremely simplified explanation attempts to show that a bitcoin address and its public and private keys all have a mathematical relationship involving prime numbers rather than trying to capture the nature of that relationship or the size of the numbers. Bitcoin uses what are called "elliptic curve algorithms" to create the public/private key pairs, but the complex math that creates them is beyond the scope of this book.

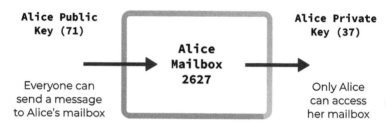

Figure 7.6: Direction of information flow in public-key cryptography

With this procedure, Bob can securely send a message to Alice, and Bob can himself publish a public key so that Alice can also send messages to Bob, enabling secret two-way communication between the two.

2.ii. Proof of Ownership

So far we've learned that public-key algorithms use a pair of keys: a public and a private one. By using Alice's public key, anyone can leave her a message that only she will be able to read, because only she has the private key. However, public-key cryptography can also be used to prove ownership of a private key without having to reveal the private key itself. As we will see in the next section, this feature of public-key cryptography allows us to digitally sign messages.

Aside from permitting her to read messages that are in her inbox, Alice's private key enables her to encrypt messages. Anyone can decrypt that message by using Alice's public key. But wait: if anyone can read her message, what's the point of encrypting it in the first place?

The reason is that this way, Alice can prove she is in possession of the private key without having to reveal the private key itself! As we will see, the same mechanism can be used to prove that Alice is the owner of specific bitcoins and Bob isn't.

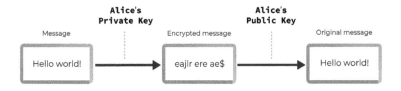

Figure 7.7: Alice can prove she possesses a private key by encrypting a text with that private key, and anyone can prove that Alice holds that private key by decrypting the encrypted message (using the public key).

3. DIGITAL SIGNATURES

3.i. Single Signatures

The traditional way to verify that a message was written by a particular sender is the document's signature. This proves a document is genuine in two respects: that it was signed by a particular individual, not an impersonator, and that the contents of the document are what the original signer intended and have not been tampered with. Can we use the methods we have just encountered to do the same digitally? This can be done by using the hash function and proof of ownership with public key cryptography, showing how cryptographic primitives can be combined for useful new functionality.

Initially, to use public-key cryptography, Alice creates a private and a public key, and makes the public key available to Bob, the recipient.

If Alice wants to digitally sign a document, she needs to do the following (as shown in Figure 7.8):[78]

1. Calculate the hash of the document.

2. Use the hash as input and encrypt it with her private key. The encrypted hash is called a **digital signature**.

3. Send the original document along with the digital signature to Bob.

What has Alice done? By calculating the hash, she has created a unique fingerprint (cf. Chapter 7.1) for the document. No other document in the world has the same hash. As the owner of the private key, only Alice can generate the encrypted hash (as described in Chapter 7.2.ii).

---

78 In practice, all these steps are automatically done by the software when Alice wants to digitally sign a document.

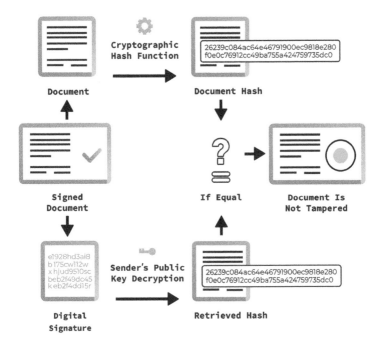

Figure 7.9: The process of validating a signed document

If Bob wants to validate the document he does the following (see Figure 7.9):

1. Calculate the hash of the document.

2. Use the sender's (that is, Alice's) public key to retrieve the hash of the document that Alice signed.

3. Compare the two hashes to see if they are identical.

If the two hashes are identical, then the message that Alice hashed and encrypted is the same as the message received. Even the slightest change to the message would result in a completely different hash. Bob can be certain that only the holder of the private key corresponding to that public key could have encrypted that message, confirming that it was Alice, and no one else, who sent the message.

By using a combination of public-key cryptography and the hash function, it is possible to recreate digitally the important features of a traditional signature. Just as with paper documents, a timestamp is often included in the message to show when the message was created and signed.

3.ii. Public-Key Cryptography and Bitcoin

In this section we explain how public-key cryptography is related to bitcoin and bitcoin addresses. Understanding how terms are connected will allow us to apply everything we learned so far to sign a bitcoin transaction.

In the previous section, we learned that public-key cryptography requires a pair of keys (private and public). Many different public-key algorithms exist. The one that bitcoin uses is called an "elliptic curve digital signature algorithm" (ECDSA). This algorithm has the nice feature that it is always possible to derive the public key from the private key, meaning that it is enough for your wallet to store only your private key, instead of a pair of keys.

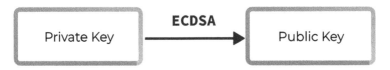

Figure 7.10: The public key is generated from the private key.

The public key is then hashed, resulting in a hashed version that is 160 bits long (about twenty-three text characters).[79]

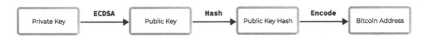

Figure 7.11: The public key is hashed.

The final step is to convert the 160-bit hash (think of 10100110000 … 101) to something that is easier for us humans to use. This step is called "encoding," which replaces groups of 0s and 1s with letters and numbers and essentially results in a bitcoin address.

Figure 7.12: A bitcoin address can be derived from its private key.

---

79 In reality, two different hash functions are applied to the public key.

The bitcoin address can be directly derived from the public key, and thus some people also refer to a bitcoin address as a "public key." However, as just explained, this is not 100 percent correct. You'll now see why the distinction between the terms is important.

3.iii. Signing Bitcoin Transactions

Having introduced digital signatures, we can now answer the questions we raised at the beginning of this section, namely how Alice can prove the ownership of her bitcoins, and conversely how Bob is prevented from spending Alice's coins.

The procedure is exactly the same as described in Section 3.i:

1. Alice owns a private key p and public key a, the public key representing her bitcoin address (as discussed in the previous section).

2. If Alice wants to send some of her bitcoin, she creates a transaction message t. In this message t, the details of the transaction are specified, like the recipient and the value of the transaction.

3. She signs the transaction message t with her private key p to generate the signature s.

4. Every bitcoin node can now validate the transaction by checking the transaction message t and the signature s, in combination with the public key a.

Note that modifying the transaction message *t* slightly to *t'* will not work, as the signature *s* would be invalid for the modified transaction *t'*. This prevents a malicious node from stealing bitcoin from Alice's account.

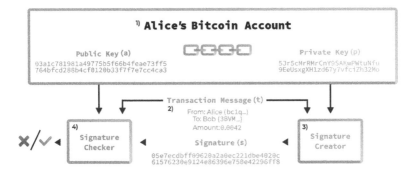

Figure 7.13: Digital signature infographic (Source: Curious-Investor, "How Bitcoin Works in 5 Minutes (Technical)," April 14, 2014, YouTube video, 5:25, https://www.youtube.com/watch?v=l9jOJk30eQs.)

The public key system is used in bitcoin to enable bitcoin owners to prove ownership in a secure fashion. Using her private key, Alice can prove that she is the owner of her bitcoins, and anyone seeking to verify her claim only needs her public key to do so. Alice does not need to reveal her private key, but nonetheless can prove her ownership of her bitcoins in an indisputable manner. In this way, the system provides both security for Alice and confidence for all users of the bitcoin network that her claim to her bitcoins is valid.

3.iv. Multiple Signatures

Advances in cryptography have made it possible to establish the bitcoin equivalent of joint accounts that can be configured to require some or all the participants to sign within a set period before the transaction expires. It would be possible now for Alice, her mother, and her lawyer to "sign" transactions jointly.

Multiple signatures create some protection against the loss of an individual private key. If, for example, two of three keys are required to sign a transaction, and one key is lost, the transaction can still go forward.

Of course, it's possible to complicate security to an unreasonable extent such that ten people, four bots, and two government agencies all need to sign off on a transaction. Here, it's necessary to find a balance between speed and security. Two-hundred-fifty-million dollars' worth of bitcoin can and should take more time to access through more complex, slower protections.

CHAPTER SUMMARY

Cryptographic hash functions produce a compact identifier from any amount of digital information. Although the smallest change in that information produces a radically different hash, the same data always generates the same hash—a hash that gives no insight into the information it represents and cannot be deconstructed to yield even a portion of the data. These attributes make cryptographic hash functions exceptionally useful for a variety of general applications including password storage and, in bitcoin, for the formation of addresses (which are bitcoin's only accounts), the security of those accounts through the use of public key cryptography, and the operation of the consensus method. Public key cryptography can be used for secure communication and for proof of ownership of private keys. These two cryptographic primitives were then combined to construct a method of digital signatures, which like traditional signatures can be used to verify both the contents of a message and that the sender is genuine.

8

BITCOIN MINING

IF, IN THE PREVIOUS CHAPTER, WE TOOK APART THE COMPO-
nents of the metaphorical car we explained how to drive, here
we'll tour the factory and see how bitcoin is made. Tempting as
it is to capitalize on the mining-for-gold metaphor, the process
is actually closer to alchemy.

Miners assemble transactions into a block and then repeat a
series of mathematical incantations until they find a combination of elements that turns their inert block into bright new
bitcoins. Thus, bitcoins are less unearthed than created the
moment the first miner solves a block's riddle, which is called
"solving the block." This alchemical process has two steps:
building a (candidate) block and solving it.

We discussed some aspects of mining in Chapter 6, and learned
that confirming transactions in a centralized system is simple
(the central "node" simply decides and all the other nodes
follow), but that things get more complicated when the system
has to be decentralized. We then discovered that a naive

approach (nodes just accept every transaction they encounter first) doesn't work, since we cannot guarantee that all participants are well-intentioned, and the network could not handle a double-spend attack. Instead of one node having full control of validating transactions (or blocks), in bitcoin special nodes (called "mining nodes") win on average every ten minutes the right to propose the next block. We will now go on to explain how this works in more detail.

1. BUILDING A CANDIDATE BLOCK

Miners create a block by selecting transactions from a pool of those as-yet unconfirmed requests that have propagated through the network. From this pool, miners select which transactions to verify.[80]

1.i. Transaction Selection

As mentioned in Chapter 6.5.iii, people initiating bitcoin transactions effectively bid on a miner's service to validate their transactions. Miners are engaged in mining to make money and preferentially select the higher paying ones. Therefore, a higher transaction fee increases the likelihood that miners will select a transaction for bundling into a block. This isn't as

---

80 Miners, in this instance, are machines that make these selections according to the rules that program them. It helps simplify already complex material to simply say that "miners select" rather than "miners are programmed to select" at the risk of anthropomorphizing the process. For the rest of this chapter, when we say "miners," please understand we mean machines, not people. We'll make a point in Chapter 8 of signaling when we use the same term to refer to the people or organizations that own the machines.

simple as choosing the highest number, however, as transactions can have different storage size requirements.

It's helpful to think of a block as a container with a set number of available spaces, like an elevator with a weight limit. If every potential customer weighs the same, the elevator operator will preferentially select the ones willing to pay the highest price for their individual tickets. Imagine the going rate for elevator rides is $9, and Alice and Bob both weigh one hundred pounds. If she's offering $10, and he's offering $9, Alice will get picked first. If, however, Alice weighs two hundred pounds and is still offering $10 to Bob's $9, Bob will get chosen because he leaves room for another $9 fare from a second hundred-pound passenger.

In the context of bitcoin transactions, the equivalent of weight in the above example is the storage size of a transaction. The size of a transaction is measured in the number of bytes necessary to store the transaction, which is variable depending roughly on the number of inputs and outputs a transaction has, inputs being bigger than outputs. A typical size of a bitcoin transaction is around 250 to 500 bytes.

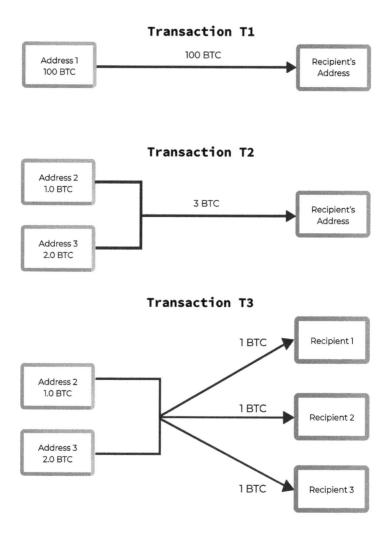

Figure 8.1: Three possibilities how inputs and outputs can be combined

In the above diagram, T1 would take up the least space in a block, as it only has one input and output, followed by T2 with two inputs and one output, with T3 with its two inputs and three outputs being the largest. This is despite the fact that T1 has the highest value in terms of the number of bitcoins transacted, as the number of bitcoins in the transaction has no influence on the transaction size, and thus the cost of the transaction.

A block holds up to one megabyte of transaction data.[81] Since more complex transactions occupy more space, they reduce the total number of transactions a miner can fit into a block. Miners usually optimize for the highest fee-*per-byte*. Like a heavier passenger, a more complex transaction needs to offer a higher transaction fee to be selected for inclusion in a block.

1.ii. The Candidate Block

Potentially, miners can select whatever transaction they like from the pool of unconfirmed transactions. However, the transactions should follow certain rules. Examples for such rules are, *inter alia*:

- If Alice has one BTC, she cannot spend more than that.

- Alice can only spend her own bitcoin (and has to digitally prove it's hers, cf. Chapter 7.2.ii).

- The bitcoin address of the recipient has to be valid (e.g., the fingerprint of a bitcoin address has to be correct, see Chapter 7.1.ii).

---

81 The block size for transaction data is limited to 1 MB. However, additional data related to digital signatures can, for certain transaction types, be stored outside of this structure (up to 3 MB), resulting in an "effective block size" limit of 4 MB (1 MB transaction data + 3 MB signature data).

Not only does each single transaction itself have to follow certain rules, but there are also rules for the block as a whole that need to be met. For example, the rules of block formation prohibit the inclusion of two transactions that "spend" the same bitcoin (the so-called "double spend" that we discussed in Chapter 6.5). Including one of the two transactions in a block is perfectly fine, but including both of them would be a violation of the rules.

As explained in Chapter 6, a valid new block not only has to fulfill all of the above rules, but also needs to include the solution for a very difficult mathematical problem. The solution is only correct if the set of transactions in the block remains unchanged, so once a block has been found, transactions cannot be added or removed from that block. As new unconfirmed transactions are received by a miner, new temporary blocks, also called candidate blocks, will be formed as long as no solution to a block has been found.

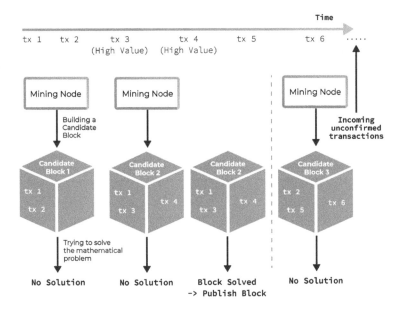

Figure 8.2: Mining nodes form candidate blocks and try to solve them.

In the above example, the miner begins with candidate block 1 with transactions tx1 and tx2, and attempts to find a solution. Before a solution is found, transactions tx3 and tx4 are communicated to the miner, which have higher transaction fees than transaction 2. If there is only space (hypothetically) for 3 transactions, the miner forms the new candidate block 2, which includes transactions tx3 and tx4 in favor of transaction tx2.[82] As a solution is being sought for candidate block 2, transaction tx5 arrives, but since its fee is not more economically attractive than those of tx1, tx3, and tx4, the miner continues

---

82 As we will see, there is no disadvantage for a miner to start working on a new candidate block compared with working on the previous candidate block.

to try to find a solution for candidate block 2. A solution is found for candidate block 2, which is then published by sending it to the bitcoin network.

Immediately afterward, the miner will continue to mine, forming a candidate block 3 by taking transactions tx2, tx5, and tx6, which remained in the pool of unconfirmed transactions.[83]

By building candidate blocks from time to time, miners can increase their transaction fee income by including more transactions and/or transactions with higher fees.

> A **candidate block** is a temporary block formed by a mining node, which includes a set of unconfirmed transactions. The candidate block and all its transactions fulfill all required rules; however, the "mathematical puzzle" has not yet been solved.

These candidate blocks (that are formed by all miners) are never published. Only after the mathematical puzzle is solved does a candidate block become a "real" block, which then is published.

---

83 If the mining node were to receive a new valid block (from a different miner), the same would happen: the node would update the pool of unconfirmed transactions and start creating a new candidate block.

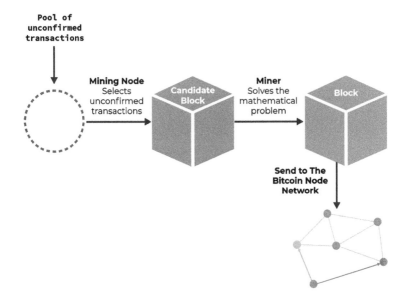

Figure 8.3: From the unconfirmed transaction pool to the bitcoin node network

1.iii. Coinbase Transaction

A block cannot be completely empty. At minimum it must hold at least one transaction. The first, and the mandatory, transaction is called the **coinbase transaction**. This is the transaction with the bitcoins that a miner earns for successfully solving a block, and has the following two components:

1. The fixed number of newly created bitcoins (the "block reward")

2. The transaction fees, which senders add in order to have their transactions included in the block

These bitcoins are sent to an address controlled by the miner, and cannot be spent until an additional 99 blocks have been mined thereafter.

The bitcoin protocol contains lots of rules, and some of them are a bit surprising at first glance. Why should freshly mined bitcoins have to wait for 99 more blocks, while all other bitcoins can be spent immediately?

The reason for this extra waiting period is related to fungibility. In rare cases (which we will discuss later) it is possible that different competing versions of the transaction history exist (so-called "forks"). After a few additional blocks, one fork will prevail while the other one will be discarded (including all its coinbase transactions). If all bitcoins were spendable immediately after the block was solved, the recipient of such a transaction would bear a risk of receiving bitcoins from the forks that later on are discarded. This in turn would mean that two types of bitcoin would exist: (a) recently mined ones, and (b) "old" bitcoins that are safe to use. As everyone would prefer bitcoin of type (b) over (a), this would inhibit fungibility. Requiring that 99 additional blocks have passed before the coinbase transaction becomes spendable ensures that all bitcoins are equally trustworthy.

An example of the transactions of a block is shown below. The first transaction (in the box) is the coinbase transaction, which in contrast to other transactions has no origin, while all following transactions come from some bitcoin address. The coinbase transaction transfers 7.0811... bitcoins to the miner (that uses the address bc1qx9t2...), of which 6.25 bitcoins are the block reward. The remaining 0.8311... bitcoins stem from the fees of the other transactions that are contained in the block (only the first two such transactions are shown below).

Block Transactions

Hash	2021-05-17 17:27
f5add697510e048bad75bccb175bc79498 dad8beb2f4dd199502e9554f902ff....	
COINBASE (Newly Generated Coins)	▶ d8beb2f4dd19959498d... OP_RETURN
Fee	7.08114266 BTC ●
0.00000000 BTC	0.00000000 BTC
(0.000 sat/B - 0.000 sat/WU - 204 bytes)	
(0.000 sat/vByte - 177 virtual bytes)	7.08114266 BTC
	2 confirmations

Hash	2021-05-17 17:17
cb175bc79498 dad8beb2f4dd9e697510 e048bad75bc199502e9dc4554f902ff....	
e697510e048bad75bc199502e9dc4	0.1863 BTC ● ▶ 87234h97510e048bad7... 856154dad8beb2f4dd19...
	0.17800000 BTC ● 0.00622082 BTC ●
Fee	
0.00214110 BTC	0.18422082 BTC
(866.842 sat/B - 323.918 sat/WU - 247 bytes)	2 confirmations
1289.819 sat/vByte - 166 virtual bytes)	

Hash	2021-05-17 17:14
eb2f4dd9e694398rhuwierfyr175bc79498 dad8bd75bc199502e9dc4554f902ff....	
b2f4dd92398rhfe98ffkiwo97510e0 bc199502e9dc457y....	16.9 BTC ● ▶ 87234h97510e048bad7... r7fgi9823rigiur83ry2ru3... 984614y98368r712uo2cj...
	0.002127580 BTC ● 0.00430959 BTC ● 0.00471013 BTC ●
	...

Figure 8.4: Block transactions (Source: "Bitcoin Block 683,980," Blockchain.com, May 17, 2021, https://www.blockchain.com/explorer/blocks/btc/00000000000000000008c-555caffd0c89a1641a9284c7969265df80ad8fa6b84.)

1.iv. The Block Header

In addition to the bundled as-yet-unconfirmed transactions, every candidate block that a miner constructs includes a block header of metadata, some of which plays a role in Satoshi's solution to the double-spend problem. This data and the bundled transactions all then become part of the new block of transactions, which gets recorded in the ledger.

The block header contains in total six fields (in total 80 bytes):

- timestamp

- previous block hash

- Merkle root

- difficulty target

- nonce

- version number

We will discuss the first three entries below and will go into the "nonce" and "difficulty" in Section 2.

The Merkle Root

A specific form of data structure is used to organize the hashes of all transactions in a block, called a "**Merkle tree.**" The details are beyond the scope of this book. However, there is an element called the "Merkle root," which is calculated using the data in a Merkle tree, much like a hash for data. This means that if a transaction in the block is changed, this will invariably also change the Merkle root. The Merkle root is included in the block header.

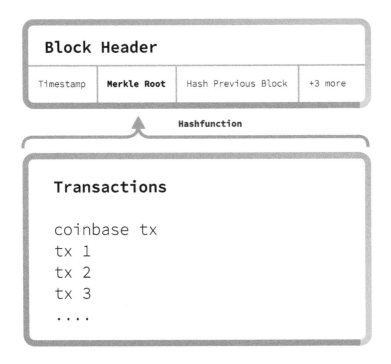

Figure 8.5: Structure of a block

Timestamp

A miner adds the approximate time the candidate block was created each time it builds one. This timestamp is used, not to time-order a block's addition to the ledger, but to allow for adjustment to the difficulty of the mathematical puzzle that miners race one another to solve (more on this in a moment). As a result, a block can enter the ledger with an earlier timestamp than the block that preceded it.

Because the miner enters the timestamp, it's impossible to verify precisely when a block was created, but two rules bracket a possible range to ensure that the time the miner records doesn't diverge significantly from actual clock time:

- The "no earlier than" rule: the time entered by the miner must be later than the median timestamps of the past eleven blocks that were added to the ledger history.

- The "not too far in the future" rule: rejects timestamps that are more than two hours ahead.

> The timestamp is used to allow for adjustment to the difficulty of the mathematical puzzle that miners race one another to solve, not to time-order a block's addition to the ledger, which is done by the hash.

Hash of the Previous Block

The data block is put into the fingerprint maker—the cryptographic hash function—which produces a digest, or hash, of the contents of the block. The hash of the previous block header must be included in the subsequent block, linking the blocks together.[84] This sequence continues, forming an ordered structure called the **blockchain**. The inclusion of the hash in the following block prevents future manipulation of the block, because if there were an attempt to change a block, it can be quickly checked that the hash of that block is no longer correct.

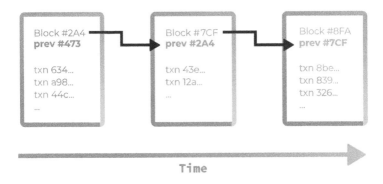

Figure 8.6: Blocks are connected by reference to the hash of the previous block.

2. BUILDING A BLOCK

Once a candidate block has been solved, the miner will then propagate this block to other nodes on the bitcoin network, so that they can use it to update their bitcoin ledger (by adding the latest block to their local blockchain). This is the next

---

84 Technically, only the hash of the block header (and not of the block itself) is calculated. However, this is often referred to as the "hash of the block." Also, the "Merkle root" is derived from all transactions of a block, and thus, any change in a block would alter the hash. Therefore, using the "hash of the block" terminology makes sense.

step in the process of achieving consensus over the decentralized bitcoin network. New blocks that are circulated between participating nodes will be checked by each node individually as to whether the block and its transactions meet all the requirements. This is part of the bitcoin mantra of "don't trust, verify," meaning that nodes do not trust each other, but verify everything on their own.

If a miner were to publish a block that violates one of those rules, the other nodes would reject this block as "invalid" (and would refuse to pass it on to the other nodes). As a consequence, the block would be rejected by the bitcoin network and the miner that published the invalid block would not receive any reward for it. Therefore, there is a high incentive for miners to stick strictly to the rules.

2.i. Too Many Blocks

Once a candidate block has been created, a complicated mathematical problem is then solved, as mentioned in Chapter 6.5.iii. The result of this is then added to the candidate block, which becomes a **solved block**. The question arises as to why this computationally expensive step is necessary, and the candidate block—which takes milliseconds to create—is not sent to the network instead.

The reason is to prevent too many blocks being circulated to the bitcoin network. If it were easy to generate a block, many nodes would do so, and there would be many equally valid blocks being sent to and circulating in the network. Because blocks take time to propagate through the network, nodes will receive blocks at different times. For example, suppose in Figure 8.7, nodes N1 and N5 start sending their (candidate) blocks B1 and B5 respectively, at the same time. The nodes N2 and N4 would see them in a different sequence (N2 would see the B1 block first, and the B5 block second, and N4 the other way around). Not being able to establish a global time-order of events would bring us back to the consensus problem, which we described in Chapter 6.5.ii.

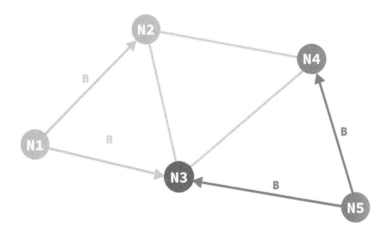

Figure 8.7: Nodes N2 and N4 receive different blocks first.

To prevent having too many blocks circulating at the same time, the process of creating a valid block is deliberately slowed down. If only one valid block is circulated at every point in time, then there is no doubt which block needs to be accepted by a node. This is the reason why Satoshi added a computationally demanding and resource-intensive step that makes it vastly more difficult to create a block.

In the following subsections we will explain what the mathematical problem looks like, and also discuss how the rare situation that two competing blocks are circulating in the network is resolved.

2.ii. Bitcoin's Mathematical Problem

We mentioned at several points throughout the book that "solving a block" requires solving a very difficult mathematical problem. Now, finally we have all the ingredients and knowledge to explain this in detail. At its core it is very simple:[85]

$$\text{SHA-2 (block-header)} \leq \text{Target Hash (Equation 1)}$$

So the "mathematical problem" is just our hash function SHA-2 (which we introduced in Chapter 7.1.i) applied on our block header with the requirement that it is smaller than or equal to something called **target hash** (often only called the **target**). The target is chosen to slow down the block production rate, such that in most cases only one block is circulating at any point in time (we will discuss the details in Chapter 8.2.v).

As we will see soon, there is a way to change the block header. Thus, the problem is to find a block header, the input of the hash function, so that the above condition (Equation 1) is satisfied.

To recall the most important properties of the SHA-2 hash function:

---

85   In reality, bitcoin applies the SHA-2 hash function twice, i.e., SHA-2(SHA-2(block header)) is calculated on the left-hand side.

- It will take some input data (in this case our 80 byte block header) and return a big integer number (the output value is between 0 and ~ 1.15×10^{77}).

- It is **deterministic** (meaning that the same input always gives the same output).

- It has the property we called the **avalanche effect**, namely that a small change in the input will lead to a completely different result (that looks like a random number).

- It is a **one-way function**: the function takes an input and finds an output, but there is no procedure to take the output to find an input.

We start with an attempt with the first trial block header, and if this is unsuccessful, we try again repeatedly with different block headers until we are successful. Of course this begs the question of how the block header can be altered. For this reason, the block header contains an extra field, called the "**nonce**" or "**nonce value**."[86] The nonce value is an arbitrary number used only once, and its purpose is to alter the block header such that the above condition can be satisfied.

So in essence all a miner has to do is the following:

---

86   Think of "nonce" as "number" + "once."

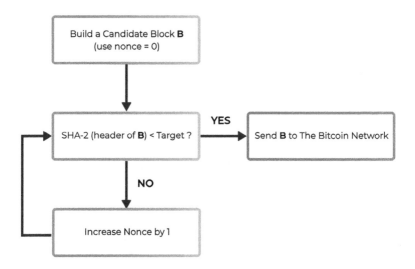

Figure 8.8: Mining Process: miners keep increasing the nonce value and calculate the hash to satisfy Equation 1. In reality miners keep changing the block header billions of times per second, so the numbers are much larger.

Because of the "deterministic" property of the hash function, a miner has to change the nonce if the previous attempt was not successful. Because of the "avalanche effect" there is no benefit of knowing that the last attempt was already "close" to the target. One nonce is as likely to be successful as every other nonce, and hence, simply increasing the nonce by one after every failed attempt is sufficient. Additionally, since the hash function is a one-way function, it is not possible to take a hash that satisfies the condition and reverse the function to find a successful nonce.

Also the search does not necessarily have to start with a nonce value of 0. Different mining nodes that start with the same value also will not do the same work twice. The reason is that miners will have their own address to receive the block reward in the coinbase transaction, which means that their respective Merkle root will be different, and hence their respective block headers. So because of the coinbase transaction miners will always be building their own individual block.

As explained above, "solving a block" is just the process of trying out millions and millions of different nonce values until one is found that satisfies the condition in Equation 1. By lowering or increasing the "target" the problem can be made harder, or easier, respectively. Because a harder problem needs more time to be solved, the target eventually allows control over the block production rate. A sufficiently low target almost guarantees that only one block is circulating at each point in time, which would solve the "too many blocks" problem we discussed in the previous subsection.

While it is difficult to find a nonce value that satisfies the condition of Equation 1, it is very easy for the nodes of the bitcoin network to verify that a block fulfills the condition. Thus, it only takes a few seconds for a valid block to be received and accepted by almost all nodes of the network.

2.iii. Hashrate

While there is some luck involved—a miner may occasionally stumble upon a valid nonce value quickly—the primary determinant of success is the ability to test as many nonce values as quickly as possible.

In a very simplified form (assuming target hash = 100), this process looks something like:

Hash (block header, nonce=0) = 1023 > 100 —▸ failure

hash (block header, nonce=1) = 7466 > 100 —▸ failure

hash (block header, nonce=2) = 1250 > 100 —▸ failure

hash (block header, nonce=3) = 85 ≤ 100 —▸ success!

In reality the involved numbers (nonce, hash, target) are much bigger and it will take more than four attempts to solve a block. Note again that going through all nonce values one by one is the only known way to find a solution. Therefore, the more combinations a miner can try out per second, the better its odds of being the first to find one that works. Each such attempt requires calculating a hash, and a miner's speed is measured in attempts-made (hashes)-per-second, also referred to as the **hashrate** and written as **H/s**.

A modern CPU can calculate around 5 to 20 million hashes per second. As hashing numbers get big very quickly, metric prefixes are used, as follows:

1 kilohash = 1 kH/s = 1,000 H/s

1 megahash = 1 MH/s = 1,000,000 H/s

1 gigahash = 1 GH/s = 1,000,000,000 H/s

1 terahash = 1 TH/s = 1,000,000,000,000 H/s

1 petahash = 1 PH/s = 1,000,000,000,000,000 H/s

1 exahash = 1 EH/s = 1,000,000,000,000,000,000 H/s

As of 2022, a modern mining machine (like Bitmain's S19) can calculate a hundred terahashes or a hundred trillion (100,000,000,000,000) hashes per second. As an indication of how difficult it is to find a block's nonce value, remember it takes the hundreds of thousands of miners across the world an average of ten minutes at this speed to solve one block!

The **hashrate** is defined as the number of hashes a miner can calculate per second and is a measure of the speed of mining.

2.iv. Proof of Work

The process of repeatedly testing numbers against the threshold is energy- and time-intensive by design. The nonce-value quest is part of bitcoin precisely because it requires so much computational effort that it slows down the entry of new blocks to the register. It is the work in **proof of work**.

Once again, because every node in the network must verify that the work has been done and has produced a valid nonce value, verification must be exponentially easier to do than the work it verifies. This disproportionality is elegantly illustrated with another military metaphor.

Imagine Simon is a commander with a thousand soldiers under his command. He calls a meeting with his counterpart in the opposing army, Teresa. Simon knows that Teresa is considering surrender, and he'd like to sign a peace treaty with no more loss of life. However, Teresa doesn't want to capitulate without a fight if there's a chance she could win.

When Simon tells Teresa he has a thousand fighters prepared to attack her encampment of one hundred, she suggests he prove the size of his forces by lining them up on the field where she can see them. Simon, not being an idiot, offers instead to prove it another way and tells Teresa to return the next morning.

Simon's army works through the night, and when Teresa returns the next day, she finds an enormous hole in the field where she proposed Simon line up his troops. Because Teresa knows there's no way even nine hundred people could make a hole that big that quickly, she signs the treaty. The hole proves the work of a thousand men over many hours, but it takes Teresa only a moment to verify it's been done. The hole itself is useless. The army didn't need a hole; it only needed to prove they'd done the work of digging one.

Likewise, a valid nonce value has no value beyond its ability to prove work was done. It proves this because the mathematical problem is posed in such a way that it's extremely hard to solve and has no shortcut. Additionally, cryptographic hash functions make a solution that is arrived at with difficulty almost trivially simple to verify. The hash of the block has to be smaller than the target hash, which can easily be checked.

This disproportionality is the same reason that proof of work is an effective spam deterrent. As mentioned in Chapter 3.3.vii, Adam Back made sending an email conditional on proof that a (much simpler) mathematical puzzle, which nevertheless required a second of the sending server's CPU time, had been solved while the receiving server could verify that the work had been done with no effort at all.

Proof of work is a system where one party proves to another party that a defined amount of (computational) work has been expended. The other party can easily verify this expenditure.

2.v. Target Hash and Difficulty Adjustments

Satoshi intentionally slowed down block creation by adding a mathematically difficult problem to the block-creation process. By choosing the "right" target hash, the block production can be limited so that on average one block is generated every ten minutes. The interval of ten minutes was chosen in order to minimize the possibility of two new blocks being released to the network at close to the same time.

This assumes that the hashrate of all miners stays the same over time. But what would happen if another miner joins and doubles the total hashrate? That would mean that twice the number of combinations can be tested in the same period of time, and thus a block would be produced on average every five minutes. With more and more miners joining, it would be only a matter of time until block production would be down to seconds, and we would be back to the "too many blocks" problem (cf. Chapter 8.2.i).

As we mentioned in Chapter 4, Satoshi correctly anticipated an "arms race" of computational speed and created an adaptation mechanism to change the difficulty of the mathematical riddle. Adjusting the difficulty might sound simple, but there are two challenges that we have to keep in mind:

1. The adaptation has to be done in a decentralized way, i.e., each node must independently be able to adjust the difficulty.

2. No one exactly knows the hashrate of all participating mining machines.[87]

Satoshi's solution to these two problems is simple and elegant. If everything is perfect, the average time between two blocks is ten minutes, and thus it should take exactly two weeks to mine 2,016 blocks (=14 × 24 × 6). If this number of blocks is already mined after one week, for example, it is very likely that the hashrate of miners has doubled in the meantime.

Every bitcoin node checks every 2,016 blocks the actual time it took to generate those blocks and compares it to the two-week goal. The target is updated as follows (slightly simplified):

$$\text{New Target} = \text{old target} \times (\text{time for the last 2,016 blocks}) / 2 \text{ weeks}$$

A few notes:

*   The time for the last 2,016 blocks can be easily estimated, as block headers have a timestamp (cf. Chapter 8.1.iv). As all nodes use the same timestamp, they will all independently come up with the same number for the new target hash.

---

87 As a decentralized system, the participating miners can be located all over the world. Not even their exact locations are known and even less so the hashrate of their mining machines.

- The target can move in both directions, e.g., if it took more than fourteen days for the last 2,016 blocks, then the new target will be higher than the old target (making it easier to find a block).

- To some degree finding a block is a matter of luck. So even if the hashrate would be perfectly constant over time the new target would go slightly up or down.

The target hash is unpleasant for humans to read, for example:[88]

0x000000000000028
16E00000000000000000000000000000000000000000000000

The target hash can be converted into a number called the **difficulty** (or **network difficulty**), which increases as the target hash decreases. The difficulty gives a relative indication how much harder it has become to solve a block. For example, if the total network hashrate increases by 10 percent, the difficulty after two weeks will go up by the same amount (and the target hash will drop by almost 10 percent, e.g., in our example in 2.iii, the target hash would become 90 instead of 100).[89]

---

88 The hash (SHA-256) is a 256-bit number. If converted into hexadecimal form (where four bits are represented by one character), sixty-four characters follow the "0x" prefix (which indicates that the following characters should be read as hexadecimal). The number is relatively small (lots of 0s following the 0x). Small numbers mean the problem is harder to solve, which in this case is an indication the network hashrate is very high.

89 1 / 1.1 = 0.9090, so 9.1% would be precise.

As of May 2021, the difficulty is about 25 trillion, and while this is still a big number, it is more accessible to humans than the target hash. Therefore, people usually talk about changes of the difficulty, instead of the target hash, and refer to the change of difficulty as the **difficulty adjustment**.

From the perspective of a miner, difficulty adjustments are important events, as they directly impact a miner's revenue for the next two weeks.[90] A miner that earned 100 BTC in one period knows that she will probably earn around 91 BTC in the coming period if the difficulty adjustment was +10%.

Figure 8.9 shows the difficulty between December 2020 and May 2021. The step-like function is a result of the difficulty being constant for about two weeks, and adjustments in both directions are possible, although the general trend is up. These charts often tell a story of what is happening in the mining industry and sometimes also of what is happening in the world:

- Due to the increase of the bitcoin price, mining became very profitable, and thus a lot of new mining machines were deployed in these six months, explaining the general upward trend of the difficulty.

- In March and April 2021, a number of major accidents in Chinese coal mines occurred, which led to safety inspections in coal power plants, necessitating their shutdown and causing large bitcoin mining operations in the region to be suspended. Thus in April

---

90   It is common to refer to the 2,016 blocks as a two-week period, although this might sometimes be a day or two off.

the hashing power of the network was significantly reduced, resulting in a large drop in difficulty, which can be seen in Figure 8.9.

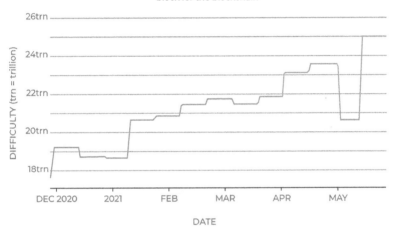

Figure 8.9: Bitcoin difficulty (December 2020-May 2021)

A few days after a difficulty adjustment has taken place, it's possible to guess what the next difficulty adjustment might be. The reason is simple: the next difficulty adjustment is based on the last 2,016 blocks, of which we already have seen a few hundred. Of course a lot can change before we reach block 2,016, but the first few hundred blocks already give an indication. It's basically the same as a survey before a presidential election; although you only ask a small number of people, you get an indication of how the race might end.

3. BLOCKCHAIN AND CONSENSUS

In the previous section we learned how a block is built and that the difficulty for solving a block is self-regulated such that, on average, blocks will only be produced every ten minutes. Slow block production ensures that in most cases only one new block will be circulating, and thus every node can update its ledger accordingly. However, in a few cases, two miners will solve a block at (almost) the same time and start relaying their block to all nodes in the network. We will solve this problem in the following section by introducing the blockchain and the rule of the longest chain.

3.i. The Blockchain

At its core, a blockchain is just a clever way to store information, in this case a transaction history.

A **blockchain** is a list of blocks and the links between them.

We have discussed blocks in great detail in Chapter 8.1 and mentioned that the block header contains the hash of the previous block (cf. Chapter 8.1.iv). This "hash of the previous block" introduces a link between them, which can be visualized as follows:

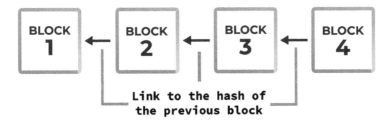

Figure 8.10: The blockchain connects blocks

The word blockchain comes quite simply from the fact that it is nothing more than blocks that are linked together in this way. The first block of a blockchain is also referred to as the **genesis block**.

A few things to note:

- If a node receives a new block, it will verify the block and then append it to the end of the blockchain (which is very simple).

- If a node needs to check the current balance of a bitcoin account, it goes through all the blocks (from 1 to 4) to see what the current balance is.[91]

- Modifying any block in the blockchain would mean that all succeeding blocks would immediately become invalid.

---

91 This might sound cumbersome, but in fact, this type of work only needs to be done once by a node (at its initialization). After that, a node will keep track of the balances (or, more precisely, UTXOs) as new blocks are generated.

The last point is important, and we will discuss it in more detail below.

For example, modifying any part of (e.g., a transaction in) block 2 would mean that the hash of block 2 changes (and thus the original nonce value would no longer solve the mathematical problem). Therefore, the "hash of previous block" field in the header of block 3 would be wrong, and updating the header of block 3 wouldn't work, as the nonce value would no longer solve the mathematical problem. Furthermore, changing anything in block 3 also means that the following block 4 would become invalid, and so on.

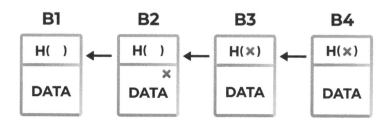

Figure 8.11: A change in an earlier block invalidates subsequent blocks.

In short: modifying any piece of information in a block means that the whole chain of blocks that follows becomes invalid. As we explained in Chapter 8.2.iii, it takes hundreds of thousands of miners (as of 2022) to produce one block every ten minutes, so creating a new series of blocks on top is extremely costly.

Immutability means the property that the contents of the blockchain are next to impossible to modify once confirmed. This property is sometimes also referred to as **tamper-proof** or **tamper-resistant**.

For this reason, it becomes more and more difficult to manipulate a transaction as the number of blocks that succeed the block containing the transaction—and that would all have to be manipulated—increases. Therefore, the likelihood that this will happen decreases dramatically, and the security of the transaction, or confidence that in fact the transaction will never be changed, rapidly becomes extremely high as more blocks are produced.

3.ii. The Longest Chain Rule

In the previous section we discussed the normal situation where blocks are appended one by one to the blockchain. However, two miners might by chance find a block at (almost) the same point in time and start circulating their blocks. We have discussed the importance of ultimately agreeing on one version of the blockchain (cf. Chapter 6.5).

So how do we solve the situation that two (or more) blocks are circulating at the same point in time? Suppose that the block 4A and the block 4B are generated at (almost) the same time, and that both are valid blocks conforming to all of the necessary rules. The situation when two (or more) blocks link to the same previous block is called a **chain split**. Let's suppose that

50 percent of the network receives the block 4A first, and 50 percent of the network the block 4B. How does the network decide which block to accept?

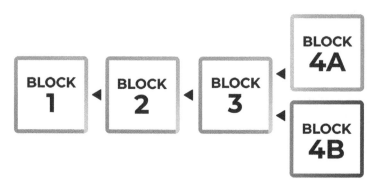

Figure 8.12: Blocks 4A and 4B are generated (almost) simultaneously.

In this scenario, the miners that encountered the block 4A first will immediately start generating blocks using that block as the previous block, and those that had the block 4B first will do the same with that block. Exactly as in the case of only one valid previous block, the miners will try to find a valid block by hashing different variants of the block header until the mathematical problem has been solved.

Suppose that a miner using the block 4A is first to find a block 5. This block 5 will then be distributed to every node in the network. If there are alternative chains available, the network will always accept as valid the "longest chain." The block sequence 1-2-3-4A-5 will be recognized as a longer chain than the other possible chain, which is 1-2-3-4B, since no block has yet been found to attach to the block 4B. All miners will now start working on a successor block to block 5. The block

4B—and the transactions within it—will henceforth not be considered part of the blockchain.

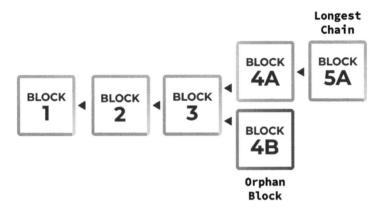

Figure 8.13: Longest chain rule

A **consensus mechanism** (or **consensus protocol**) denotes a mechanism that ensures that a distributed system (such as bitcoin) eventually reaches consensus. Bitcoin's consensus mechanism is called Nakamoto consensus.

The **longest chain rule** (also referred to as **Nakamoto consensus**) stipulates that all nodes accept the longest chain as the valid version of the blockchain. This means that everyone in the network can agree on the same blockchain (and thus the same transaction history).

There is a (very small) chance that the situation will repeat itself, and that again both for the block 4A and the block 4B valid blocks are found using both blocks as previous blocks.

In this case this process will repeat, until miners working on one side of the chain can successfully distribute a block to the whole network before a block from the other side is found.

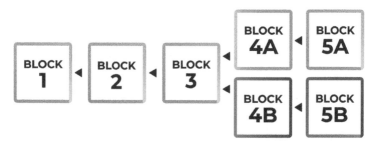

Figure 8.14: Blocks 4A and 4B both have subsequent blocks 5A and 5B.

In practice, since the sizes of the parts of the network receiving the different competing blocks are unequal, the block being received by the larger part of the network will have more computational power applied to solve the mathematical problem and is therefore much more likely to find a valid block before the smaller part of the network.[92] This inequality makes it vanishingly unlikely that competing chains will persist for long.

Furthermore, since bitcoin's block size is comparatively small relative to the bandwidth and network speed (of the order of 1–2 MB), blocks are transmitted quickly, reducing the possibility of having two blocks circulating at the same time.

---

92   This is because in practice, two competing blocks are not produced at *exactly* the same point in time, and thus, one block will have a small head start propagating itself.

Making the assumption that the probability of two blocks being published at the same time is 2 percent, the probability of this happening twice in a row is 2% × 2% = 0.04%, and so on for three in a row (0.0008%).[93] Therefore the probability of a sequence of two simultaneously released blocks very rapidly becomes tiny. As soon as only one of the two branches finds a block, the other miners will all switch over to the longest chain, abandoning the blocks 4B and 5B in the example below.

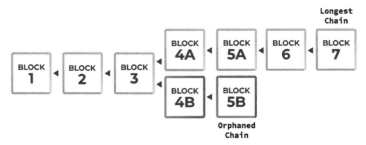

Figure 8.15: Longest chain rule

It is important to understand that the miners of any orphaned block (e.g., 4B and 5B in this case) will *not* receive the block reward for these blocks, despite having worked hard and finding a correct solution. The reason is that the block reward is only spendable if another 99 blocks have been mined on top (cf. Chapter 8.1.iii), which is not the case for blocks 4B and 5B.[94]

---

93 Although, research suggests it is much lower (Aat de Kwaasteniet, "Miners, Block Time and Orphans, A Trinity," *Coinmonks* [blog], Medium, January 5, 2020, https://medium.com/coinmonks/miners-block-time-and-orphans-a-trinity-680f45f8dd42).

94 Assuming a small miner would continue mining another ninety-nine blocks on this orphaned chain 4B (but it does not become the longest chain), the coins would be spendable but only within the orphaned chain. Since all nodes respect the "longest chain rule," they would completely ignore what's going on in the orphaned chain, and thus, the coins from 4B are practically useless.

Not benefiting from mining on an orphaned block is a very strong incentive for miners to immediately switch to the longest chain (and not waste valuable resources on an **orphaned chain**, sometimes also referred to as **stale blocks**).

It is this combination of the "longest chain rule" and the economic incentive system that guarantees that ultimately only one chain will prevail and consensus will be reached.[95] Reaching consensus is not deterministic, but becomes rapidly more likely with each block that is added to the blockchain.

When a node receives a new chain with more cumulative computational work than the one it currently has, it discards the blocks that are not in the new chain, and replaces them with the blocks in the new chain that the node did not yet have. This is called a **blockchain reorganization**.

3.iii. Confirmations

In Section 3.i we discussed that a transaction in a block is safer if several blocks were already added on top of that block. And

---

95   The longest chain rule, as described by Satoshi in his white paper, was quickly adjusted to become the blockchain on which the most computational work has been proved to have been performed. This is to prevent attacks, for example, by starting a local alternative chain just before a difficulty increase and manipulating the time-stamps on the alternative chain so that the blocks appear to be taking longer than the ten-minute target, which will cause the difficulty to decrease. This would ulti-mately enable the attacker to create a longer chain than the main chain, at which time he could broadcast it to the main network and have his chain accepted as the valid chain, with the main chain being discarded.

in Section 3.ii we deepened our understanding that for short periods of time short "competing" blockchains can exist that will quickly resolve by the "longest chain rule."

To describe how safe a transaction is, the bitcoin community uses the following terminology:

An **unconfirmed** or **pending** transaction is a valid transaction that has been submitted to the bitcoin network, but that has not yet become part of a block.

Once a transaction is in the latest block, it is said to have one **confirmation**. With each block subsequently attached, it receives an additional confirmation.

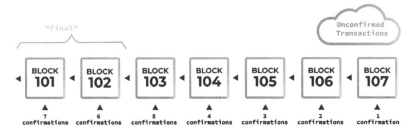

Figure 8.16: Confirmations and the blockchain

As a convention, a transaction is considered as finalized or completed if it has six confirmations, although in practice even one confirmation is very secure. In theory (see Section 3.ii) no transaction is absolutely final, but after six confirmations, the probability that the network will reverse this transaction is vanishingly small.

Transaction finality means that it is practically impossible to alter or reverse a transaction in the blockchain. For bitcoin, six confirmations are considered to be final.

3.iv. The 51 Percent Attack

In section 3.ii we explained how the "longest chain rule" ensures that ultimately one blockchain will prevail. We assumed so far that all participants are honest (mining) nodes, and thus it actually doesn't matter which chain will be the longest in the end. The goal is to ensure that consensus is reached and that double-spend attacks can be prevented. The mechanics we described in 3.i and 3.ii ensure this if all miners are honest.

However, what happens if not all miners are honest? In this section we describe the degree to which the system is resilient against dishonest mining nodes, and what kind of damage a malicious miner could cause.

What Is a 51 Percent Attack?

We recall from 3.ii that all bitcoin nodes will consider the "longest chain" to be the one valid blockchain. That is, all transactions that are in the blocks 4A to 7A are considered to be valid, while the ones in 4B and 5B are not.

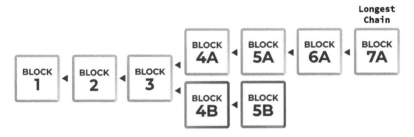

Figure 8.17: Longest chain

As an example, let's think about the example we introduced in section 3.ii explaining the longest chain rule. The longest chain A is at the top, containing blocks 4A through to 7A. Taking that state as a starting point, what would be the consequences if a malicious actor were to publish blocks 6B, 7B, and 8B?

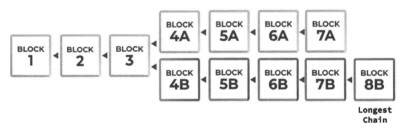

Figure 8.18: The longest chain changes side.

The bitcoin network would realize that the chain with the B blocks is now the longest, and therefore the valid chain. All the transactions that are in blocks 4A to 7A, but not in blocks 4B to 8B, would be reverted. All the transactions in the B blocks would be valid. Suppose a malicious miner named Mallory had deliberately made a transaction that had been part of a block in chain A, but not in chain B, and received a good or service in return. After publishing chain B she would have received that good or service for nothing, since the transaction paying for it would become invalid. Since Mallory is able now to spend these coins in the transaction for a second time, this is referred to as a "double spend." Additionally, she would receive the block rewards from the blocks 4B to 8B.

So how can the honest nodes stop Mallory from producing blocks 6B to 8B? They can't! While mining blocks is very hard and requires a substantial investment in mining machines and electricity (cf. Chapter 6.5.iii), Mallory will eventually succeed in producing blocks 6B to 8B and publish them. However, during the time that Mallory is busy working on her version "B" of the blockchain, the honest miners will continue their work on the longest known chain (7A) and will add further blocks, e.g., 8A to 15A. So by the time Mallory publishes 6B to 8B, the honest nodes have produced a much longer chain, and Mallory's evil plan is foiled.

But is it possible for Mallory to produce more blocks than the honest nodes? Theoretically yes. If Mallory produces blocks faster than the honest nodes she will eventually win, even if she starts a few blocks behind.

Mining a block means solving the complicated mathematical problem (cf. Chapter 8.2.ii), and we learned that solving this problem comes down to trial and error. If one nonce doesn't work, try the next and so on. So if Mallory manages to try out more nonce combinations per second than everyone else (i.e., having a higher hashrate than everyone else combined), she will produce blocks faster and eventually win the race for the longest chain. In other words: Mallory needs at least slightly above 50 percent of the total hashrate to do this.

A **51 percent attack** (or **majority attack**) refers to a potential attack by a miner (or a group of miners) that is in control of the majority (> 50 percent) of the network's hashrate in a proof-of-work system. An attacker would have the ability to rewrite the history of blocks and thus be able to reverse transactions.

What Can a 51 Percent Attacker Do?

We saw that Mallory can double-spend her coins if she controls at least 51 percent of the hashrate. She can also always force her blocks to be in the longest chain (while the other blocks, e.g., chain "A," become "orphaned").

A 51 percent attacker can do the following:

- Double-spend transactions

- Prevent other miners from mining any valid blocks (because the attacker produces blocks faster than everyone else, blocks by other miners will become orphaned)

- As a consequence, prevent transactions from going into a block[96]

---

96 that never belonged to Mallory.

An attacker can't:

- create additional bitcoins (except for the block reward), or

- send coins that never belonged to them.

You might wonder why Mallory is not able to steal coins from addresses controlled by others. The reason is that in order to form valid transactions she would need the private keys belonging to those addresses, which she does not have. Even as a malicious miner, she still needs all the transactions in her blocks to be valid, otherwise the rest of the bitcoin network will not accept her blocks and would continue to consider chain A to be the valid chain.

Is Bitcoin at Risk?

As discussed above, an attacker (or group of attackers) can cause huge harm to the bitcoin network. However, there are three things to consider:

1. **Building mining infrastructure on such a scale is extremely expensive.** As of mid-2021 an attacker would at least need 2,000–3,000 MW of electricity and mining equipment to come even close to performing such an attack. The cost of building such a gigantic mining farm would certainly be in the USD billions.

2. **The reward for attacking a blockchain is a one-off economic benefit.** An attacker can double

spend or will mine all future blocks. However, a
51 percent attack will quickly be noticed by other
participants. As soon as this is the case, trust in
the chain is broken, and the value of the coin will
massively drop.[97]

3. **Mining honestly is economically more attractive.**
   An honest miner will receive block rewards and
   transaction fees for a long period of time and in most
   cases will generate a profit.

A 51 percent attack, while theoretically feasible, is not economically advantageous. Our attacker Mallory would need to invest
billions of dollars to acquire that much hashing power. And if
she did and were successful, her success would result in bitcoin
losing its value. She would have spent enormous amounts of
money to steal something that her success devalued. It would
be like stealing paper money by setting it on fire.

> **Incentive structure for miners:** the system is designed to
> reward honest mining, and discourages dishonest behavior.

Because attacking bitcoin is so expensive and dishonesty
will not pay, there has never been a successful 51 percent
attack on bitcoin. However, some much smaller cryptocurrencies, e.g., "ethereum classic" and "bitcoin gold" (not to be
confused with ethereum and bitcoin), were attacked in the

---

97 Thus, an attacker would probably put a short on bitcoin, i.e., place a bet on drop-
ping market prices.

past.[98] There are two major differences between these coins and bitcoin:

1. Because they were both much smaller, the capital investment needed for an attack was much lower.

2. The same hardware (GPUs) could be used to mine other coins (e.g., Ethereum) as well.

To elaborate on the second point: bitcoin mining hardware (which is optimized to calculate the SHA-2 hashing algorithm) is practically only useful for bitcoin mining and pretty much useless for every other task. So building mining infrastructure for an attack on bitcoin will result in a complete write-off of that hardware, if the attack was successful and the bitcoin value plummets. In contrast, GPUs are used to mine various coins, including Ethereum, and therefore the mining hardware used for an attack could be economically beneficial to continue to mine one of these other coins, as well as being able to be used for calculation tasks outside of cryptocurrencies (such as machine learning applications or rendering images for a video clip).

The possibility remains that actors may decide to perform a 51 percent attack for reasons other than direct economic gain. Take, for example, the scenario that a state or supranational

---

98   Zack Voell, "Ethereum Classic Hit by Third 51% Attack in a Month," Coindesk, last modified September 14, 2021, https://www.coindesk.com/markets/2020/08/29/ethereum-classic-hit-by-third-51-attack-in-a-month/; Jack Martin "Bitcoin Gold Blockchain Hit by 51% Attack Leading to $70K Double Spend," CoinTelegraph, January 27, 2020, https://cointelegraph.com/news/bitcoin-gold-blockchain-hit-by-51-attack-leading-to-70k-double-spend.

organization may perceive bitcoin as a significant threat to its fiat currency and initiate a 51 percent attack to defend it. Nevertheless, given the vast resources required to do so, this is not likely in our opinion.

In July 2014, the mining pool (a loose group of miners) GHash.io briefly reached more than 51 percent of the overall hashrate. While GHash.io did not have bad intentions, it raised major concerns within the bitcoin community. In the end Ghash.io voluntarily promised to not exceed 40 percent of the overall hashrate. By 2015 GHash.io fell below 2 percent and since then no mining pool has reached that hashrate level.

While most people primarily are concerned about a miner (or a group of miners) reaching 51 percent, things already start to get dangerous if an attacker has 30–40 percent of the overall hashrate. This is for two reasons:

1. While an attack with >51 percent of the hashrate is practically certainly successful, there is still a limited chance for an attack with a hashrate below this threshold. For example, by controlling 40 percent of the total hashing power, the chances that a miner can double spend by mining six blocks faster than the other miners is 25 percent. That's not a guarantee of success, but it's dangerous when millions of dollars are on the table.

2. At around 33 percent of total hashing power, a miner can carry out a complex strategy known by

the name of **selfish mining**, which can compel other miners to have to follow his chain.[99]

Even if an attack on bitcoin could potentially start at lower levels (like 33 percent), we have to keep in mind that the investment required is still in the billions of dollars and the potential gain is comparatively small. So for the same reasons we discussed before, a rational miner will always decide to be honest.

3.v. Summary

We presented the process of how the bitcoin network reaches consensus as to which transactions are included on the block-chain in a decentralized manner. The precondition is that the majority of the miners are honest. The threat to the network if a malicious miner did control the majority of the hashing power does in principle exist, but the massive cost, as well as the incentive structure, preclude such an attack in practice. As of June 2021, bitcoin in its more than decade-long history has never suffered a successful attack, and we believe it is now robust enough that this will not occur.

---

99   Ittay Eyal and Emin Gün Sirer, "Majority Is Not Enough: Bitcoin Mining Is Vulnerable," *Communications of the ACM* 61, no. 7 (July 2018): 95–102, https://doi.org/10.1145/3212998. Normally, miners have a strong incentive to immediately publish a new block. However, in a selfish mining strategy, the miner does not publish the new block and tries to mine another block on top of it in secret (so he would be in possession of two valid blocks kept for himself). If another miner publishes the first block, the selfish miner would publish the two blocks he kept private before and thus have published the longest chain. As a consequence, the miner that published only one block would not get the block reward. If the selfish miner has around 30–40 percent of the overall hashrate, he would harm the other miners so much that they would have an economic incentive to join the selfish miner, thus bringing him toward 51 percent.

4. THE ECONOMICS OF MINING

Miners are the guardians of the bitcoin network: they protect the network and ensure consensus. However, miners do not do this out of altruistic motives, but because they are profit-seeking participants. Bitcoin's smartly designed incentive structure ensures that the best economic interests of the miners are also in the best interest of the network. In this section, we will go deeper into the reward system and the economics of mining.

4.i. Mining Income

Miners who successfully solve a block receive the block reward and the transaction fees for the transactions in that block (cf. Chapter 8.1.iii). Getting these rewards is the reason why miners invest into mining hardware and electricity.

Mining Income = Block Rewards + Transaction Fees

Block Rewards

From bitcoin's inception in 2009 through November 2012, the block reward was defined to be 50 bitcoin per block. On average blocks are found every ten minutes, which is equivalent to 144 blocks per day, or 7,200 bitcoins that were produced every day. We discussed that Satoshi designed bitcoin to be scarce and that the maximum amount of bitcoin that can ever be produced is 21 million.

If miners were to mint 7,200 new bitcoins every day, there would be no upper limit to the number of bitcoins. To ensure a hard 21 million limit, Satoshi introduced the "block halving" event. That means that every 210,000 blocks (approximately every four years) the block reward halves.

> A **block halving** denotes the event that the block reward halves, which happens approximately every four years.

The first halving happened in November 2012 and resulted in a block reward reduction to 25 bitcoins per block. When the halving happened, 10.5 million bitcoins (= 50 percent of the total amount of bitcoins) had already been minted by miners. The next halving happened in July 2016, resulting in a block reward reduction to 12.5 bitcoins per block (after another 25 percent of the bitcoin were mined).

Original Block Reward: 50 BTC

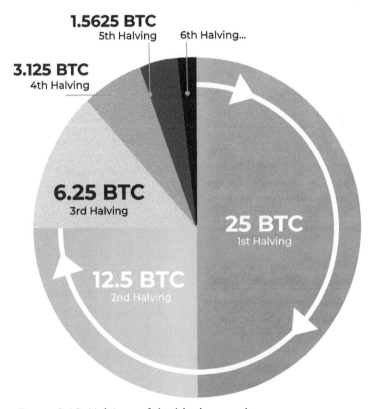

Figure 8.19: Halvings of the block reward

This is much like a small child's version of slowly eating a delicious chocolate cake: you eat one half of what's left. And then again a half of what is left after that, and so on. You would never finish eating the cake. However, in bitcoin the pieces of the cake are limited by its smallest unit (the "Satoshi"). Thus the last fractions of a bitcoin will be minted around the year 2140. However, long before that miners will only mine a few hundred Satoshis per block.

Halving	Date	Block Reward (in BTC)	Total Coins Mined	Total Coins Mined %
Bitcoin launch	Jan 3, 2009	5050	0	0%
1st halving	Nov 28, 2012	25	10,500,000	50%
2nd halving	July 9, 2016	12.5	15,750,000	75%
3rd halving	May 11, 2020	6.25	18,375,000	87.5%
4th halving	Expected March 2024	3.125	19,687,500	93.75%
5th halving	Expected 2028	1.5625	20,343,750	96.88%

Figure 8.20: Bitcoin halving and block rewards

The reason why the time periods are a bit shorter than four years is because the total hashrate of the bitcoin network has increased over time, and thus the block times are on average a little bit shorter than ten minutes. After 2,016 blocks (around two weeks) the difficulty adjusts to the increased hashrate, but the previous blocks were already mined at a faster rate.

Transaction Fees

When doing a transaction the sender can also specify how much he or she is willing to pay in transaction fees. Miners are incentivized to select the transactions that generate the highest fee income for them (cf. Chapter 6.5.iii and 8.1.i). The miner earns the sum of all transaction fees in a block (and the fees are part of the coinbase transaction).

For example, the miner of block 691905 received 6.25 BTC as a block reward, and in addition the fees of all (in total 3,000) transactions adds up to 0.31836788 BTC. The sum of the block reward and the transaction fees (6.56836788 BTC) is then sent as part of the coinbase transaction to the address bc1q7wedv4 ... 99mukymc.

Block Reward	6.25000000 BTC
Fee Reward	0.31836788 BTC

Block Transactions

Hash	9e697510e048bad75bccb175bc79498 dad8beb2f4dd199502e9dc4554f902ff...			2021-07-20 20:53
	COINBASE (Newly Generated Coins)	▶	d8beb2f4dd19959498dad8b eb2f99502e9dc4554f902ff...	6.56836788 BTC ●
			OP_RETURN	0.00000000 BTC
			OP_RETURN	0.00000000 BTC
			OP_RETURN	0.00000000 BTC
				6.56836788 BTC
Fee	0.00000000 BTC (0.000 sat/B - 0.000 sat/WU - 375 bytes) (0.000 sat/vByte - 348 virtual bytes)			1 confirmations

Figure 8.21: Block rewards in the coinbase transaction

The transaction fees that miners earn each day can change significantly over time as the chart below shows (average over thirty days).

Total Transaction Fees (BTC)

The total BTC value of all transaction fees paid to miners.
This does not include coinbase block rewards.

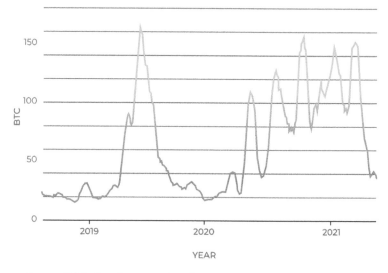

Figure 8.22: Total transaction fees

Long-Term Considerations

The block halving event, which reduces block rewards by 50 percent, occurs approximately every four years, and thus block rewards are pretty predictable from a miner's point of view. However, ultimately the block reward will be zero, and long before that block rewards will be practically negligible in the sense that they won't be valuable enough to sustain large mining operations, which are needed to keep the bitcoin network secure.

So who is going to pay miners in the long term so that they can secure the network? The idea is that the transaction fees will

increase over time as more and more people are doing transactions in bitcoin, and will be sufficient to pay for network
security.

In the beginning when there were very few (and low fee) transactions, and the bitcoin price was low, the block reward incentivized miners. Until mid-2016 transaction fees were only
responsible for about 1 percent of a miner's income. In 2021,
this number increased to about 5–10 percent, so transaction
fees indeed are becoming more important over time.

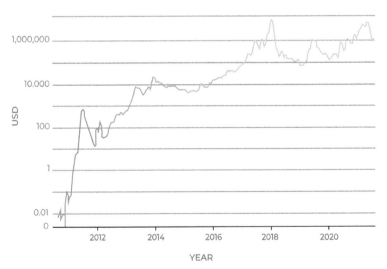

Total Transaction Fees (USD)

The total USD value of all transaction fees paid to miners. (30-day avarage)
This does not include coinbase block rewards.

Figure 8.23: Total transaction fees

The fees are not only increasing in relative terms, but also in absolute USD value. While daily transaction fees only amounted to less than a hundred-thousand dollars per day in 2014–2016, they usually reached a million dollars in 2021 (also thanks to the increasing bitcoin value).

The situation is a bit of a "tragedy of the commons": everyone would like to use a secure network, but no one is willing to (voluntarily) pay for it. Bitcoin ensures a minimum level of transaction fees by limiting the block size (cf. Chapter 8.1.i). As the above chart shows, this system works very well for now, but it will take a few more halvings of the block reward to know for sure if this will continue.[100]

4.ii. The Network Hashrate

The income from mining allows people around the world to run mining machines (which in turn secure the bitcoin network). Some people only run one mining machine, while some companies run hundreds of thousands. Each machine has a certain hashrate, and the sum of the hashrate of all machines is called the **network hashrate**.

---

100   Dan Held, "Bitcoin's Security Is Fine," Medium, May 15, 2019, https://danhedl. medium.com/bitcoins-security-is-fine-93391d9b61a8; Raphael Auer, "Beyond the Doomsday Economics of 'Proof-of-Work' in Cryptocurrencies," Globalization Institute Working Paper 355, Federal Reserve Bank of Dallas, February 2019, https:// doi.org/10.24149/gwp355; Miles Carlsten et al., "On the Instability of Bitcoin without the Block Reward," *CCS '16: Proceedings of the 2016 ACM SIGSAC Conference on Computer and Communications Security* (October 2016): 154–67, https://doi. org/10.1145/2976749.2978408.

Estimating the Network Hashrate

The "problem" with the network hashrate is that no one knows its exact value. Miners can directly measure how many hashes per second their machines try out but not how many other miners have attempted in the same period.[101] In fact, we do not even know how many mining machines are in use, where these mining machines are located, or whom they belong to.

However, the network hashrate can be estimated by using the difficulty. Remember the difficulty D (cf. Chapter 8.2.v) is precisely defined, universal for all bitcoin nodes, and constant for roughly two weeks. The average hashrate H for such a two-week window can be estimated as:[102]

$$H = D \times 2^{32} / 600$$

For example, the network difficulty as of July 29, 2021, was approximately 13,672 billion, which as per the above formula results in 97.87 EH/s (an Exahash is 10^{18} hashes).

During a two-week time frame, the hashrate can change as miners add or remove machines, and an estimate based on a two-week period will not consider more recent effects. However, to find the hashrate for a period of time shorter than two weeks is more problematic. To improve the estimate, one would need to consider the current block production rate.

---

101   And even that number is not exact.

102   This formula is a very good approximation and good enough for all practical purposes.

For example, if blocks are produced every eleven minutes on average (instead of every ten minutes), one could assume that the network hashrate is about 10 percent lower than the above formula suggests. However, over short periods of time, chance plays a more important role in determining the block production rate. It's like rolling a die, and sometimes you roll three sixes in a row, and then for the next twenty rolls no sixes at all.

If we observe a small block sample size (like the 144 blocks that are produced on average every day), this kind of probabilistic effect has an impact on the overall result. The chart below (which is based on estimating the hashrate from the last 144 blocks) shows huge jumps of up to 30 EH/s within a single day, which are a result of "luck" and not of miners switching their machines off and on. For this reason, using the production rate of blocks over periods of time shorter than two weeks leads to less accurate estimates of hashrate.

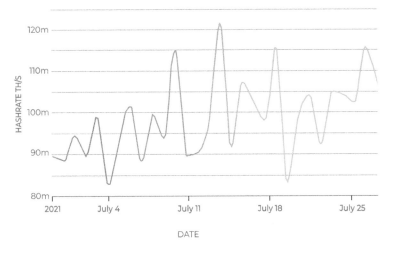

Total Hash Rate July 2021 (TH/s)

The estimated number of terahashes per second the bitcoin network is performing in 24 hours.

Figure 8.24: Total hashrate in July 2021

The Hashrate Explosion (2009–2020)

The hashrate has increased more than a trillion-fold between 2009 and 2019.[103] This increase can be attributed to two main factors:

1. The number of mining machines has grown over time.

2. The hashrate of each machine has increased.

---

103 A trillion is a million million, or 1,000,000,000,000.

Mining "Satoshi Style" (2009–2010)

In its early days (2009–2010), people mined bitcoin on their home computers with a normal "central processing unit" ("CPU"). These computers are typically running at a hashrate of a few MH/s. It is very likely that Satoshi Nakamoto used a CPU for mining bitcoin, as well.[104]

By the end of 2010, the bitcoin network hashrate reached about 100 GH/s, which means that a few ten thousands of computers were mining bitcoin at that point in time. The CPU miners are sometimes referred to as the "first generation of bitcoin miners."

GPUs for the Win (2010–2013)

In May 2010, Laszlo Hanyecz (the same person who bought pizza for 10,000 bitcoins, cf. Chapter 4.2.i) published an algorithm that allows using a "graphics processing unit" ("GPU") for mining bitcoin. GPUs are primarily used to accelerate graphics-intense computer games, as well as for commercial graphic applications. However, their ability to work on hundreds of tasks in parallel is also advantageous in many other areas, such as in machine learning or bitcoin mining.

The advantage: a GPU runs at a few hundred MH/s and thus is about one hundred times faster than a normal CPU (while

---

104   Sergio Demian Lerner, a cryptocurrency security consultant, found some evidence that Satoshi used one high-end CPU and some optimizations to mine about 1.1 million bitcoin [Sergio Demian Lerner, "The Patoshi Mining Machine," *Bitslog* (blog), August 22, 2020, https://bitslog.com/2020/08/22/the-patoshi-mining-machine/].

using approximately the same amount of electricity). This technological innovation and an increasing interest in bitcoin fueled the first "hashrate explosion," which resulted in the network hashrate going up by about a factor of a thousand and reaching between 10–20 TH/s by 2012.

Total Hash Rate (TH/s)

The estimated number of terahashes per second the bitcoin network is performing in the last 24 hours

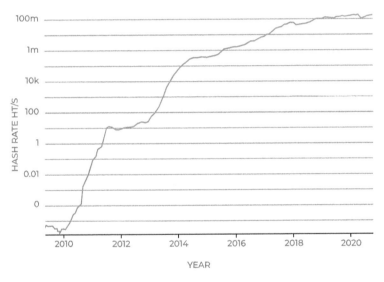

Figure 8.25: Total hashrate

Since using GPUs gave miners such a huge advantage over CPUs, the entire industry was forced to upgrade. This became the "second generation of miners." Running a CPU was no longer economically viable. This type of "arms race" for faster and more efficient machines was practically inevitable, with a repeating pattern of new technology becoming available and almost completely replacing its predecessor as the dominant type of mining equipment.

The Rise of the (ASIC) Machines (2013–2014)

In early 2013, the third generation of bitcoin mining started when the first specialized mining chips were manufactured. Instead of running the SHA-2 mining algorithm as software on a CPU or GPU, the SHA-2 code is hard-wired at the chip level. These types of chips, which are customized for a particular use case (such as bitcoin mining), are referred to as "application-specific integrated circuits" ("ASICs"). ASICs are extremely fast and efficient for the specific task they were designed for but can do practically nothing else.[105]

The first ASIC miner, "Avalon Miner" (Avalon A3256), was about 50–100 times more efficient than a typical GPU, and also the cost per GH/s was much lower than for a GPU.

The introduction of ASICs caused another "hashrate explosion" that led to an increase from 20 TH/s (early 2013) to about 300 PH/s by end of 2014. So in just two years, the hashrate grew by more than four orders of magnitude. Just as the use of GPUs ended the commercial use of CPUs for mining, the availability of ASICs in turn put an end to bitcoin mining with GPUs. By the end of 2014, probably more than a million machines distributed all over the world were hashing nonstop to find the "right" nonce value.

---

105 An old bitcoin ASIC has almost zero value, while a GPU that cannot be used for bitcoin mining anymore still has other use cases, e.g., playing games.

Continuous Growth (2014–2020)

In the following years, chip technology constantly improved. Not only did the chip designs get better, but the mining manufacturers were also able to pay for better chip-processing techniques, which basically means having more and smaller transistors on the same chip area. This is sometimes referred to as the **process node** and is an indication of the size of the transistors.[106] First generation ASIC chips were using a 110 nm (nanometer) process node, while modern ASICs use 7nm technology (and thus can hold about one hundred times more transistors in the same area).

Placing more and smaller transistors in the same area helps in two ways: (i) reducing the cost for hashrate and (ii) being more energy efficient. For example, the first Avalon miners (2013) were consuming about 6,000 watts of electricity to keep the miners running at 1 TH/s. As of 2020, a Bitmain S19 miner can achieve the same hashrate at 30 watts, an improvement by a factor of 200. At the same time, the cost per TH/s to purchase the miners dropped by a factor of 500!

Between 2014 and the end of 2020, the network hashrate increased from 300 PH/s to about 135,000 PH/s, so about three orders of magnitude again. The reason is mainly the ongoing improvement of mining (and in particular chip) technology. However, the value of bitcoin also went up significantly (bitcoin traded at about USD 300 at the end of 2014, and only six years later it reached USD 30,000). The price appreciation meant that bitcoin mining was extremely profitable and,

---

106   Note that the naming convention in chip technology (e.g., "16 nm") does not refer to the size of the transistor itself but only to a small part of it.

as during the California Gold Rush, miners all over the world raced to join in, starting or scaling up their participation.

To return to our army general (cf. Chapter 8.2.iv), in the absence of faster soldiers (or a backhoe), additional troops are the shortest route to a bigger hole, particularly if they dig in different parts of the field. With one miner trying out nonce values starting at 1 and working upward, and another one starting at 1 billion trillion and working down, they will never duplicate any work. Having thousands of miners working in concert to essentially dig in different parts of the field delivers a significant speed advantage. Huge mining farms can host over one hundred thousand machines, and by the end of 2020, there were approximately ten million machines distributed all over the world, keeping bitcoin safe.

4.iii. Mining Costs

As explained in the previous section, bitcoin mining became a huge and very profitable business. Most mining farms are run by professional companies to make a profit. In Section 4.i we discussed the income side of a mining farm. From a cost perspective there are two components for building and operating a mining farm:

1. "Capital expenditure" ("CapEx")

2. Operating costs

Capital Expenditure

Typical capital expenditure includes buying the land and facilities to house the miners (e.g., warehouses or containers), the mining units themselves, substations and transformers, high voltage power cables, and cooling equipment. Of these, the biggest cost is by far the miners.

A **substation** is a part of the electrical distribution system that transforms power from high voltage (e.g., 115kV or more) to medium voltage (typically 2kV–30kV).

Operating Costs

The computational power required to calculate trillions of hashes per second is extreme and energy-intensive. The miners themselves use a tremendous amount of electricity, with more consumed to keep them cool. This kind of extraordinary energy use involves more than extension cords and a hefty electricity bill. Once a mining farm is up and running, it also incurs ongoing costs, such as taxes, the salaries of technicians and maintenance workers, management, administration, and security costs. However, by far the most significant operating cost—typically around three-quarters of the total cost—is electricity. To maintain a competitive advantage, mining companies will thus search for and use the cheapest available electricity sources.

Miner Efficiency

Because electricity costs are so important, miners will constantly check whether it makes sense to upgrade their mining equipment to more energy-efficient machines.

If, for example, it costs Alice $4,000 worth of electricity per hour to power enough miners to earn the equivalent of $8,000 every hour, she'll enjoy an excellent profit. It would make good economic sense, under these conditions, for Alice to keep mining and perhaps even to invest in additional miners. If, however, the cost of electricity rises or the value of bitcoin falls, Alice's operation becomes less profitable. If it begins to cost her more to produce a bitcoin than it does to buy one, she'll probably stop mining. At this point, Alice might use the money she'd been spending on electricity to buy bitcoin rather than mine it.

For example, if the electricity costs $4,000 and the revenue is only $4,000, she would not make any profit at all. At this point in time Alice might decide to invest in new mining equipment that produces the same amount of hashrate, but consumes far less electricity. Let's assume the latest generation of hardware consumes 50 percent less electricity: that would reduce her hourly costs to $2,000.

The ratio of energy consumption to hashrate measured is called the **efficiency of a miner**. Let's look at some examples:[107]

---

107 Sometimes, the efficiency is expressed in different units; all of the following are equivalent: "kW per TH/s" is the same as "W per GH/s" is the same as "J per GH."

Mining Device Comparison

Miner	Release Date	Consumption (kW)	Hashrate (TH/s)	Efficiency (kW per TH/s)
Avalonminer A1	2013	0.6	0.072	8.333
Bitmain S9	2016	1.13	11.5	0.098
AvalonMiner 1066	2019	3.25	50	0.065
Bitmain S19	2020	3.25	95	0.034

Figure 8.26: Comparison of bitcoin mining devices

The hardware improvements are remarkable (cf. Section 4.ii). For instance, in 2019 an Avalon miner produced 50 TH/s while consuming 3,250 Watts, and only about a year later the S19 delivered almost twice the hashrate while consuming the same amount of electricity.[108]

Mining Dynamics

If the bitcoin price appreciates, then Alice's revenue will increase, while her costs remain unchanged. She and other miners are then incentivized to invest in more miners, raising the network hashrate. In reverse, the same logic applies, with a lower bitcoin price reducing the profits of miners. Miners whose profits turn into losses may drop out, causing

---

108   For reference, the average American consumer consumes about 3,000 kilowatt hours (kWh) per year. A Bitmain S19 miner running nonstop would consume 28,500 kWh in the same time, so, on average, as much as nine to ten US households.

the hashrate to fall. Everything else being equal, miners are sensitive to the bitcoin price, and the hashrate will follow price movements.[109] The hashrate itself, however, does not have a direct effect on the bitcoin price.

> Hashrate doesn't drive the price, but the price can drive the hashrate.

Block halving has a highly disruptive effect on the economics of mining, as revenue halves from one moment to the next. Miners who were barely profitable before a halving will run at a loss afterward and are very likely to drop out. However, because the timing of this disruption is known and anticipated well in advance, investment in mining equipment will take this into account.

4.iv. Geography

Because a substantial part of the electricity used by miners is spent on cooling the machines, the colder the environment, the less expensive it is to mine for bitcoin. Consequently, many large mining operations have chosen to set up or move north. Alternatively, very inexpensive electricity can offset a warmer environment. China, for example, having invested heavily in coal-burning power plants, has an over-supply of cheap electricity. This, combined with the fact that one of the largest

---

109   This ignores other significant factors, such as the introduction of improved hardware and block-reward halving.

manufacturers of ASIC miners is located there, made China an attractive place for bitcoin mining operations, until it banned cryptocurrency mining in mid-2021.

Readily available hydroelectric power has also been a draw. Places like Washington State in the US, Quebec in Canada, and several locations within Russia have become competitive bitcoin mining locations.

Large mining operations frequently buy energy upfront—often up to two years in advance—to hedge against future changes in electricity prices. If the price of bitcoin drops so dramatically that it's no longer profitable, miners who have such a contract in place won't save anything by turning off their machines. This is one scenario where miners would continue to operate despite incurring losses.

An additional level of challenge is that mining operations generate income in bitcoin but must cover their costs in fiat currency (most often in US dollars). Thus, in addition to the speed and efficiency of miners, large-scale mining operations also closely monitor the cost of electricity and the price of bitcoin.

CHAPTER SUMMARY

Because bitcoin is decentralized, the tasks of validating transactions and operating the choke points of Satoshi's groundbreaking consensus mechanism fall to members of the network—specifically to those members who operate specialized nodes called miners.

Miners select transactions optimizing for price per bit and build them into a block, which screens out any mutually exclusive transactions. To ensure that new blocks are added to the blockchain slowly enough to keep the number of chain splits small, miners must solve a very hard mathematical problem.

Since this work is deliberately (and provably—hence the term *proof of work*) time- and energy-intensive, the first miner to solve each new block is rewarded with new bitcoins, which are created for (and only for) that purpose. The maximum amount a miner can earn per block reward is set and falls by half approximately every four years. The system rewards honest miners when they perform their role in reaching consensus in the decentralized network.

There are large financial incentives to mine bitcoin, causing enterprises to invest in large facilities to do so. The major cost is the electricity to power the mining machines themselves and their supporting equipment, which leads to geographical concentrations of the industry in locations offering low-cost electrical power sources. A miner's revenue is a function of the price of bitcoin in fiat currency and the network hashrate.

The bitcoin blockchain unifies without centralizing. It is the ultimate arbiter of truth. With identical and constantly updated duplicates of itself on every node, it is both a shared memory and a linear history. As such, its formation is governed by a set of principles that protect it against fragmentation. The longest chain rule makes it next to impossible for forks created simultaneously to continue beyond a few blocks. It eliminates the final opportunity for a coin to be spent twice, while the linkage of each block to every other makes the chain extraordinarily resistant to tampering.

CONCLUSION

HAVING CONCLUDED OUR INTRODUCTION TO BITCOIN AND the blockchain—the deepest part of the rabbit hole—we hope to leave you confident in your understanding not only of the bitcoin wonderland, but also the scope of its evolution and the underpinnings of its construction. Bitcoin is spearheading a monumental shift from a centralized to a decentralized world, which has the potential to impact not only money, but, for example, supply chains; contracts in the financial, real estate, and any other industry; the internet of things; and decentralized decision-making.

Decentralized proof of ownership is one promising application that has been pursued in various forms, with projects as varied as decentralized land registries, decentralized ownership of characters in computer games, and digital and real-world art (often referred to as non-fungible tokens, or NFTs). With proof of ownership administered on a blockchain, transactions can be carried out with that property in the same way that bitcoin is transferred. Decentralized financial services are also available, with borrowing and lending being organized without the need for a bank or other financial institution as an intermediary.

Within the monetary domain, however, by the time this math-assisted evolution occurred, decades had passed since anyone could cash in paper money for Fort Knox gold. When bitcoin was invented, most money was already digital—for every ten dollars in the US economy, there was less than one physical dollar bill.

At the same time, the relatively new internet was bringing together people with common interests from all over the world. In one such group dedicated to technology-based privacy as a path to social and political change, a conversation began about how many of the internet's virtues—the lack of a central authority and the possibility of anonymity prominent among them—might be brought to money.

The person (or people) styled "Satoshi Nakamoto" put together a white paper posted to the cypherpunk group. In it, they proposed "a peer-to-peer electronic cash system" that would function as both a currency and a payment system based, at its most fundamental level, on the idea that time (or effort) is money. Under this system, in very broad strokes, miners create value by doing something difficult that requires the expenditure of physical energy, similar to digging for gold.

Like gold, bitcoin is scarce. Moreover, it is also carefully designed to be divisible, durable, portable, and fungible. Most importantly, bitcoin is decentralized. It was designed from first principles to be a better form of money, and to carry out the function of money more efficiently. The engineering behind bitcoin is sophisticated and technical, but not beyond an interested layperson's grasp. We think it is worth understanding, as money is a critical part of our daily lives and historically many currencies (e.g., the denarius) were debased and/or collapsed. We believe that bitcoin and other cryptocurrencies have a strong chance of becoming a significant pillar of the financial system in the upcoming years and decades, and are thus worth studying in some depth.

Our goal in writing this book was to provide readers enough grounding in the terms, definitions, and history of money to appreciate the origins, agenda, structure, and operation of bitcoin. To us, it represents the most paradigm-shifting technology since the invention of the internet. To those who understand bitcoin as we hope you now do, it offers not just a state-free currency but a new way of conceptualizing money that is as radical as it is elegant. We hope you feel confident about further exploring bitcoin and are inspired by what it means and offers. We want as many people as possible to learn about and understand this new form of money.

For us, understanding bitcoin begins with an overview of money's history, learning its traits and function, and getting a grasp of payment systems. Having learned what makes money most useful, it will be interesting to see whether governments remain the main driving force behind its improvement. For the first time, there is a digital form of money with the characteristic of being decentralized, affording the opportunity to ascertain how beneficial this attribute is in this context.

Bitcoin is a radically creative impulse beautifully personified in the mysterious figure of Satoshi Nakamoto. His remarkable innovation fundamentally changes the way we think about money. His creation was engineered to meet human and economic needs and to out-perform by many metrics all the currencies and payment systems that had come before it. Still, for all its engineering, bitcoin is remarkably easy to use. As long as they take adequate care to protect their private keys, people can buy bitcoin from an ATM as easily as they can order an Uber.

Thus, in much the same way a person can drive without knowing much about how a car works, people can participate in bitcoin without knowing anything about cryptographic hash functions or blockchains. However, to enjoy driving, to handle higher performance vehicles or race them, you need a bit more insight into their design and mechanics. Likewise, we believe that understanding—if not the operations within the black box of hash functions—how they're deployed in bitcoin will enhance your experience of using it. In part, this is because they are so foundational.

Bitcoin uses cryptographic hash functions for the proof of work that creates new coins, the addresses that establish their ownership, and the public-key cryptography that secures them. All this, of course, is recorded in what is, functionally, the heart of bitcoin—its blockchain. Blockchain technology has implications beyond bitcoin and cryptocurrency for arenas as diverse as music, medicine, and voting. It creates links between each bit of data it holds and every other in a tamper-resistant system that can be both extraordinarily powerful and completely decentralized. Understanding how it operates can increase your insight into the rapidly evolving future of many different aspects of the world above the rabbit hole and beyond the matrix.

We envision a world where everyone can participate in (and benefit from) a decentralized monetary system. We intended this book as an effort to educate you about bitcoin and its advantages—knowledge being an indispensable precondition to the confident adoption of new technology. If you found this book valuable and it helped you to understand bitcoin, we have together gotten closer to making that world a reality.

GLOSSARY

51 Percent Attack: An attempt to co-opt the blockchain by adding new blocks to a new chain so quickly (requiring at least 51 percent of the total network's speed) that it outpaces the original longest chain. A 51 percent attack could be used to double-spend coins.

Asymmetrical Cryptography: Codes that use one key to encode the cipher and a second one to unlock it.

Austrian School: An economic school of thought that favors a marketplace where people can choose between different and competing forms of money. Adherents of the Austrian School, such as Friedrich Hayek, believe that a free market will eventually choose the most stable money.

Bank Run: (also called a **run on the banks**) A feedback loop in which bank customers, attempting to withdraw their deposits, overwhelm the bank, prompting worries about the bank's solvency, driving still more people to withdraw their funds and thus increasing the probability of default. This in turn creates additional anxiety among customers, leading to more withdrawals until the bank ceases to allow further withdrawals, or the system collapses.

Bitcoin Account: → Bitcoin Address

Bitcoin Address: A unique alphanumeric sequence twenty-six to thirty-five characters long, roughly analogous to a bank account's routing number. A bitcoin address allows a user to receive and send bitcoin. Example: bc1qye7x0y42eumyyxwz8vmler06ljuwdx7agvvqjy

Bitcoin Ledger: → Blockchain

Bitcoin Wallet: An app that manages a user's public bitcoin addresses, as well as the associated private keys.

Block: A data structure that is composed of the block header and the actual transactions. Each block is linked to its predecessor, together forming a blockchain.

Block Header: Metadata added to the bundled transactions which includes (among other things): information about the difficulty level under which the block was solved, a timestamp, the previous block's hash, the Merkle root, and the nonce value that solved the block.

Blockchain: A database that records the creation and every transaction of all existing bitcoins and is housed and regularly updated on every node in the bitcoin network. Also known as the "bitcoin ledger."

Checksum: The output of a hash function, typically twenty to sixty-four characters long, which can be used to check the correctness of a file or a bitcoin address for modifications. Synonyms: fingerprint, hash.

Coinbase Transaction: The first transaction in each block, which includes the bitcoin address to which the transaction fees and block reward should be directed.

Commodity Money: Money whose value is derived from the underlying commodity, e.g., cigarettes.

Consensus Mechanism: A method for reaching consensus within a decentralized system. Bitcoin uses Nakamoto consensus, which means that a node should trust the "longest chain."

Cryptocurrency: A digital currency that uses strong cryptography and a decentralized control system.

Cryptocurrency Exchange: A company that operates a platform, stores both fiat money and cryptocurrencies, and organizes interactions among people who want to trade one for the other.

Cryptographic Hash Function: A complex mathematical operation that maps an arbitrarily long input to an output of predetermined length (typically around 32 bytes). The (short) hash can be used as a unique identifier for an input, much like a fingerprint is a unique identifier for a person.

Cryptographic Primitive: A well-established, elementary cryptographic algorithm that is often used in cryptographic protocols. This means that for decades, the algorithm could not be broken by the cryptographic community, important for building a secure system.

Cypherpunk: A believer in the use of strong cryptography to ensure privacy despite the widespread use of digital technology.

Digital Signature: A means to confirm the authenticity of a message transmitted via a digital medium, typically using public-key cryptography and a hash function.

Double-Spend: When it is possible, by mistake or fraud, for one unit of currency to be spent twice. A payment system should not allow double-spends.

Fiat Money: A currency that is issued by an authority at will, with no physical or other external backing (fiat—Latin for "let it be done").

Fingerprint: → Checksum

Fractional Reserve Banking: A system of banking where banks hold only a fraction of their depositors' assets and lend the rest.

Fungibility: A trait of money that enables one unit to be interchangeable with any other of the same value.

Genesis Block: The first block on a blockchain.

Gresham's Law: The monetary principle that "bad money drives out good money." If one of two (or more) nominally equivalent representations of value is factually devalued, the more valuable form tends to be hoarded and is found less and less in general circulation.

Hashrate: The number of hashes (attempts to find a nonce value) made per second; used as a measure of processing power.

Keynesian School: A branch of macro-economic theories that favors, among other things, monetary policy executed by a central bank.

KYC (Know Your Customer): A set of rules ensuring financial businesses collect and verify information about their customers.

Legal Tender: A currency merchants in a given jurisdiction are legally required to accept as payment.

Medium of Exchange: An intermediary instrument used to facilitate trade by serving as an agreed-upon standard of value for transactions.

Merkle Root: The top node of a Merkle tree, which combines all underlying data of the tree in a single hash. In bitcoin the Merkle root represents all transactions of a block, and is included in the block header.

Merkle Tree: A tree-like data structure where the leaves represent transaction hashes. Branches in the tree are hashes of the child branches (or leaves). Also sometimes referred to as a "**hash tree**." A Merkle tree allows efficient and secure verification of the underlying data.

Mt. Gox: An early bitcoin exchange based in Japan, which processed about 80 percent of all trades. Funds were stolen from Mt. Gox and the exchange collapsed in 2013. The downfall of Mt. Gox is considered to be one of the most high-profile crypto hacks.

Node: A computer of the bitcoin network that runs the bitcoin software. Each node stores the whole blockchain and verifies all blocks and transactions.

Nonce Value: The "Number Only Used Once" (NONCE) is a parameter in the block header that can be changed arbitrarily in order to change the hash of a block header. To receive the block reward, miners need to find a nonce such that the block meets the difficulty restrictions.

Open Protocol: A protocol is computer code that governs the rules of a network. Protocols may be public or proprietary, but any computer that follows them can participate in the network. All of bitcoin's protocols are public, making it an open protocol.

Open Source: Source code is the foundation of software. Software that is open source can be studied and modified by anyone. The bitcoin software is open source.

Payment System: A method of transferring monetary value.

Peer-to-Peer: Most frequently used to describe the interaction of computers within a network. Any peer-to-peer structure allows for direct interactions between participants without the need for a hub or centralized mediation. One well-known example is BitTorrent.

Peer-to-Peer Transaction: A transfer of monetary value between individuals that requires no mediation.

Pseudonymity: The use of pseudonyms rather than (real) names to identify individuals and accounts.

Representative Money: Money that uses some material (e.g., a paper slip) to represent some form of commodity money (usually coins/precious metals). A gold certificate is an example of representative money.

Satoshi Nakamoto: The pseudonym used by the person or people who developed bitcoin.

Satoshi: The smallest division (one one-hundred-millionth) of a bitcoin. Named after the inventor of bitcoin.

Script: A piece of programming code that carries out a specific function. Each transaction in bitcoin is in fact a small script.

Security: In payment systems, a measure of how difficult it is to create illegitimate transfers of value by means of theft, counterfeit, or fraud.

Smart Contract: A contract between parties that is both defined and enforced by an algorithm / computer program.

Store of Value: The property of money that makes possible the trade of goods and services across time and place.

Symmetric Cryptography: Uses the same key to both encrypt and decrypt sensitive information.

Timestamp: An approximation of the time a block was created. Included in its block header and used for adjustment to the difficulty level.

Transaction: The transfer of monetary value.

Unit of Account: The trait that allows money to account for and compare the value of different goods and services. Also called "**Measure of Value**."

Validation: A bitcoin node checks each block, including all transactions within it, to ensure that all rules are met. This check is called "validation" and allows a node to trust a block without having to trust the miner who created that block.

ACKNOWLEDGMENTS

MANY PEOPLE HAVE HELPED US IN A NUMBER OF DIFFERENT ways in the writing of this book. Writing a book about bitcoin has been a very rewarding, but also challenging task, and the support we have received has been invaluable. We would like to sincerely thank those who have helped us create and improve our book.

Linda Häusler and Katharina Haid were both reliable and tireless in their organization of the many meetings we needed in the course of the book's preparation, coordinating seamlessly between various people and time zones while taking into consideration often very busy schedules. Kayla Sokol and Darnah Mercieca ensured that the project kept moving and that all the components were held together throughout.

Skyler Grey helped us enormously in taking what can be a fairly technical topic and transforming it so that the subject became engaging and accessible, enhanced by her willingness to study the subject deeply.

Where would a book be without illustrations? Tassilo Hansen and Helen Eriksson created the original graphics in this book, taking often complicated ideas and procedures and turning them into graphics so that the reader can visualize as well as read what is happening. Boris Matesic and Goran Markovanović created the spectacular and very fitting cover design.

Dr. Kristian Haehndel suggested the succinct and very appropriate title of the book, and has also been a strong and inspiring partner and friend to us in our various cryptocurrency endeavors.

Jihan Kahssay provided invaluable legal advice, ensuring that the content matter of the book adhered to the law in relevant jurisdictions.

David Jefferies, Dr. Richard Jefferies, Tom Lane, and Xenia Muth all took the time to read early drafts of the manuscript and provided detailed and thoughtful feedback on both the content and the use of language in the book. The corrections and comments received helped to greatly improve the book, ensuring that it is as accessible, comprehensible, and well structured as possible.

Anthony would also like to thank his girlfriend, Katarzyna Kulczycka, for her loving support and patience during the long period of writing the book. Marco Krohn would like to thank Amalia for her valuable input. In addition, he is grateful to his wife, Jihan, for her love, support, and her hilarious comments. She showed great interest in his work, and came up with an innovative suggestion on how to explain the blockchain. Marco Streng would like to thank his girlfriend, Valeriia Kovalchuk, and his brother, Timo Streng, for corrections throughout the book.

ABOUT THE AUTHORS

MARCO KROHN STUDIED MATHEMATICS, PHYSICS, AND economics, obtaining a PhD in theoretical physics and working for an investment bank for several years after graduation. After learning about bitcoin, Marco quit his bank job to join the cryptocurrency revolution. He is the co-founder of many successful blockchain companies, including Genesis Digital Assets, the world's largest mining company, Genesis Mining, and Genesis Group.

Anthony Jefferies studied mathematics and engineering and completed his PhD in the field of numerical simulation of combustion. He worked for more than ten years at major German car manufacturers, performing computational fluid calculations in the research and development division. Since discovering bitcoin, he has been involved in a number of cryptocurrency projects, including a cryptocurrency exchange and the development of quantitative tools for bitcoin data analysis.

Marco Streng is the co-founder and CEO of Genesis Digital Assets, one of the largest industrial-scale bitcoin mining companies in the world. In 2013, Marco was studying to become a mathematician when he first discovered bitcoin. He became fascinated by the technology and assembled his first bitcoin miner in his dorm room before rapidly expanding and building industrial-scale mining farms around the world. Before Genesis Digital Assets, Marco co-founded Genesis Mining and Genesis Group.

Zoran Balkic has been a computer scientist since he was a child, studying then teaching computer science at the university level for fifteen years. His first bitcoin project in 2013 involved using SMS to buy bitcoin, and he went on to found and lead successful companies in the cryptocurrency industry. His interest in education continues, and he is an active participant in the Croatian bitcoin community.

Printed in the USA
CPSIA information can be obtained
at www.ICGtesting.com
LVHW071947250823
756235LV00058B/49/J